The Horse and Pony Book

SALLY GORDON

TREASURE PRESS

First published in Great Britain
by Octopus Books Ltd
for W H Smith & Son Ltd

This edition published in 1983 by
Treasure Press
59 Grosvenor Street
London W1

© 1980 Octopus Books Ltd

Reprinted 1984

ISBN 0 907812 25 2

Printed in Hong Kong

Contents

1 At the riding school

Most people learn to ride at a riding school and for many this can also provide an introduction to the daily routine care of horses and ponies. The term 'riding school', however, embraces a multitude of different types of establishment. At one end of the scale there are numbers of small, usually country or rural-based, places that keep no more than a few ponies out at grass and where the standard of instruction is often not very high. At the other end of the scale there are the very large, highly organized centres where many valuable horses and ponies are kept stabled and where instruction is given by very well-qualified people. In between these extremes there are all sorts of other establishments keeping varying numbers of animals, some of which may be stabled and others kept at grass. Tuition will be offered to differing standards.

Although all reputable riding schools will have properly trained and experienced people to look after their horses and ponies, many are prepared to let keen novice riders help in general daily work and routine, often in return for some extra riding tuition. Even if tuition is not offered as reward for such hard labour, it is a particularly useful and worthwhile way of learning about stable management and horse and pony care, since the knowledge gained is practical rather than theoretical.

Choosing a school

The choice of a riding school is extremely important, both for learning to ride and for becoming familiar with the basic aspects of caring for horses and ponies. Obviously it will be governed to a large extent by the schools established in the area where you live, but generally there will be at least two or three from which to choose. Make enquiries about all of them before deciding on any particular one. Find out how many horses and ponies they have and the condition in which they keep

Bustling activity throughout the day is part of every busy stable yard.

A row of horses observe the goings-on in the yard outside with varying degrees of interest!

them. Find out, too, how many experienced grooms work at the stables and whether they are prepared to take on inexperienced help. If the first place you look at has several scruffy horses and ponies crowded together in one muddy, churned-up field with a few ramshackle stables and everything comes under the care and guidance of just a couple of people, this is not the place to offer your services.

You can tell a great deal about the way the establishment is run from your first impressions on walking into the stable yard. If it looks clean, neat and tidy, if the horses are well groomed and look alert and healthy, if the grooms are well turned out and cheerful-looking (although do not expect them to look super-smart and spotlessly clean – their job is often a messy one, as you will discover) and if there is a general air of happiness and efficiency, then it is likely to be a well-run establishment of a good standard. If, on the other hand, the yard looks as though it has not been swept for weeks, if it is full of dull, listless-looking ponies covered in mud and sweat stains and tied to broken fences, and if the grooms look dirty and

disconsolate, this is a place to avoid.

If you feel your first impressions have not told you all you need to know, you can carry your observations a little further. Look inside the stables. Have they been mucked-out that day, so that the bedding is clean and sweet smelling, or is there, instead, a strong odour of ammonia? Do the horses look contented as well as healthy, or do they flatten their ears and back away as you approach the door of their stables? Check the tackroom, too. The saddles and bridles should be neatly hung up and stored, with the leather looking clean and supple, not dirty and cracked. The room where the food is kept provides another pointer to the type of establishment. It should be clean and well swept, with the food kept in lidded containers. The various feedstuffs should smell sweet and pleasant, not old or musty.

Becoming a helper

If you are satisfied by all these things that the school is a reputable one likely to give you a good basic knowledge in horse-mastership and horse management, find out if and when they would like you to help. The duties and daily chores that are the routine of all riding schools and with which you will be expected to assist are outlined in the

following pages. But first, perhaps, it might be sensible to consider the clothes you should wear. Strong, tough jeans of some sort, boots or strong shoes (depending upon whether you will have to tramp across muddy fields), and a shirt, jumper and anorak (depending on the weather) should be all you need until you begin to ride.

Catching a pony

It is probable that the school you have selected and which has agreed to let you be a 'helper' will be a fairly small one, with most of the ponies used for the daily rides kept out at grass. The first chore of the day, therefore, will be to catch them and bring them into the yard to prepare them for a ride.

Ponies and horses vary considerably when it comes to allowing themselves to be caught. Some will come willingly, always it seems, pleased to see and serve their human master. Others never like to forsake their comparative freedom and remain shy and difficult to catch throughout their lives. One thing is certain – if the only time a horse or pony is caught is when he is going to be

ridden, he will soon become difficult to catch. He will associate being caught only with work and the best way to avoid that is just not to be caught. For this reason, it is important to make a habit of catching up a pony from time to time just to make a fuss of him, have him shod, or groom him before turning him out again.

If a horse or pony is known to be difficult to catch, turning him out wearing a headcollar can be a help. This way there is no need to take a headcollar into the field with you, so the animal is usually less suspicious as you approach him. However, it is much better not to turn a horse out wearing a headcollar. The leather straps can, however well oiled, rub and chafe his head and they can also get hooked up on a low branch or fence post as the horse rubs himself.

The correct way to go about catching a horse or pony is to go into the field, shutting the gate behind you, with the headcollar over one arm. Hold it behind your back if the animal is shy and take a titbit of some sort with you. A piece of bread, a carrot, an apple or a

Approach a pony directly but quietly when you go to catch him. A bucket of food should help.

handful of nuts are the most acceptable. Avoid giving the time-honoured lump of sugar, which is as bad for horses as it is for humans. Walk quietly but directly towards the animal, talking to him gently and calmly. If he allows you to come straight up to him, offer the tit-bit and as you do so slip the rope of the headcollar round his neck, standing on his left or nearside. By doing this, should the pony decide to move away before you have buckled on the headcollar, you have some hope of restraining him. Slip the noseband of the headcollar over the pony's nose. Bring the strap over the top of the head and buckle it.

Having caught the animal, you now have to lead him back to the yard. Unless there is some good reason for not doing so, horses and ponies should always be led from the nearside. Hold the rope close to the headcollar with your right hand, taking up the surplus in your left hand so that you do not trip over it. Then lead the pony towards the gate, walking quietly by his side, level with his shoulder. Do not try to drag him along if he is reluctant to follow – in any tug-of-war between you the pony is bound to win. Instead, encourage him to move by talking gently and, if necessary, giving him a tap on his hindquarters.

If there are other ponies in the field that are not being caught up at the same time, they may well follow you to

RIGHT: After catching a pony, be very careful not to let others out of the field as you lead your pony through the gate. BELOW, LEFT and RIGHT: Loop your arm round the pony's nose to hold him while you put on the headcollar.

Do's and don'ts

Don't rush into the field, leaving the gate swinging open behind you.

Don't run towards the pony, shouting and waving your arms as you approach.

Don't chase after the pony if he begins to walk or trot away from you. He will always be able to move faster than you can.

Do use a headcollar, not a bridle, to catch and lead the pony. A hard, cold bit pushed into the mouth is neither a pleasant or a gentle introduction to the start of a day's work.

Do lead the pony quietly out of the field back to the yard. If you run to the gate, this will excite any other animals in the field and you could soon have a stampede on your hands. In addition, it will churn up the ground if it is at all wet.

Do take a bucket or bowl of nuts if you know the pony tends to be difficult to catch. You can rattle this to attract his attention and it is more enticing than a hand-held titbit.

Do talk to the pony quietly as you approach and catch him. Pat and make a fuss of him to show that you are pleased.

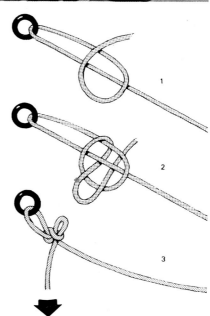

How to tie a quick release knot.

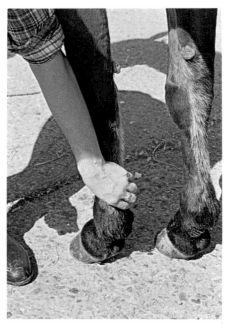

the gate, in which case you must be careful not to let them get out as you leave the field. Shoo them away as you approach the gate, then open it quickly and lead the pony through, holding the gate all the time. Make sure, too, that the gate is firmly latched behind you.

If you have to walk along a road back to the yard, walk on the right hand side of the road facing the traffic and keeping the pony tucked well into the side. You are then positioned between the animal and any cars that pass and if he shies or jumps, he is likely to do so away from the road rather than into it. However, a pony should not be led on a road by the headcollar. He should have his bridle on.

If a horse or pony is to be tied up in the yard (as opposed to being shut in a stable or loose box) a quick release knot should always be used. Such a knot can be undone instantly just by tugging on the free end if an emergency arises which demands the quick release of the pony. Also make sure that you tie the pony to something firm, preferably to a correctly positioned tethering ring secured into the wall. Do not choose a rickety fence post or one of the stable drainpipes, which is likely to give way if the pony pulls back sharply.

There are several ways of tying a quick-release knot. The one illustrated is simple and effective. To release it just pull on the end of the rope. If the pony jerks his head, however, the knot will hold fast and remain secure.

Picking out feet

Having brought the pony into the yard and tied him up, he must now be got ready for the day's work. Some grooming will be necessary, but horses and ponies kept out at grass do not need the thorough grooming given daily to those that are kept stabled. The aim in this instance is to make the pony look clean and neat for the day's rides but not to brush it so much that the grease is removed from its coat. This grease is essential to grass-kept animals, par-

ticularly in the winter, since it helps to keep the coat waterproof and the pony warm.

The first thing to do, then, is to pick out the pony's feet. This is to remove any mud or stones that may have become lodged in the feet and may cause pain or discomfort when out for a ride. Use a hoof pick and begin with the nearside foot. Stand facing the pony's tail and run your left hand down the leg until you reach the fetlock (see diagram, page 94). Squeeze the joint gently, saying 'Up' to encourage the pony to lift this foot. Most horses and ponies, in fact, will do so automatically as they become familiar with the routine. Carefully clean the underneath of the foot, working the hoof pick down towards the toe, being particularly careful not to hit, and so bruise, the frog (see diagram, page 108). This is the only sensitive part of the foot that is exposed, but it is a very important area. Make sure the groove either side of it is quite clean.

Work round the pony, picking out each foot in turn. The hind legs are picked up in the same way – that is, by running your hand nearest the pony down the leg to the fetlock and squeezing this gently to encourage him to lift the leg. Stand well to the side when lifting up and picking out the hind legs, so that if the pony does lash out, he will not strike you. After this, wash all the mud and dirt off the outside of the hooves, using the water brush. This not only improves the pony's appearance, but also allows you to inspect the hoof and shoes more easily to see if the clenches have risen, which indicates that it is nearly time for reshoeing.

Brush away any dried mud or sweat marks from the coat and legs, using the dandy brush. Make sure, in particular, that the area under the saddle and girth are quite clean, for any bits of mud or sweat left there can soon rub into a sore from the pressure of the saddle and the weight of the rider. Again, when brushing the hind quarters and legs, stand slightly to one side just in case you touch a sensitive spot and the pony lashes out. Never kneel by the side of a pony when brushing the lower legs. You are not in a position to move quickly if anything frightens him and he jumps sideways. If the mud on the

CENTRE and LEFT: Squeezing the fetlock tells the pony to lift his foot. Work carefully down to the toe with the hoofpick. TOP: Use a damp sponge on the corners of a pony's eyes but always be very gentle.

pony's body or legs is very wet, it is better to leave it despite appearances. Brushing will spread it further.

Unbuckle the headcollar and do it up round the pony's neck, leaving his face free for brushing. Use the body brush on this area (the dandy brush is too harsh) and be very careful not to hit the protruding cheek bones or hurt the eyes. Use the body brush also to brush the mane and tail. Again the dandy brush is too harsh and tends to break the hairs. Brush the mane thoroughly to one side, starting at the top of the neck and brush the tail by standing slightly to the left as you face the hindquarters, holding the tail in your left hand and brushing out a strand or so at a time.

Sponge the eyes and nostrils with a clean sponge wrung out in fresh water. Then oil the hooves and the back of the heels with hoof oil. This gives some protection against wet and muddy conditions as well as smartening the overall appearance.

Those frequent occasions when it rains all through the night will present you with a very wet, as well as very

muddy, animal. The best thing to do is to remove the worst of the wet and mud using a sweat scraper. Pull the edge of the curved surface gently over the coat, then rub the coat all over with large handfuls of dry straw. This will also help to remove much of the wetness. Always rub the way the coat lies not against it, since this will just rub the wetness into the skin. After that, cover the pony's back with fresh, dry, straw and put a large piece of sacking on top. Buckle a surcingle round the pony's middle to keep everything in place. The purpose of this is to dry completely the animal's back. A saddle should never be put on to a wet coat as it will tend to rib the skin more quickly. However, the straw should not be left on the pony's back for more than an hour or it will begin to make him hot and uncomfortable.

Rub down wet, muddy, legs with handfuls of straw, then let the mud dry before brushing it off with the dandy brush. Dry the ears, too, using either straw or a stable rubber. When the ears are more or less dry, pull them very

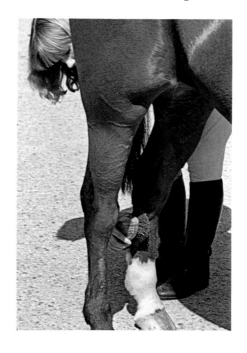

ABOVE: You should hold the pony's tail while brushing dried mud off his hindlegs. BELOW: If a pony is very dirty he can be hosed down – but only do this on a hot, sunny, summer's day.

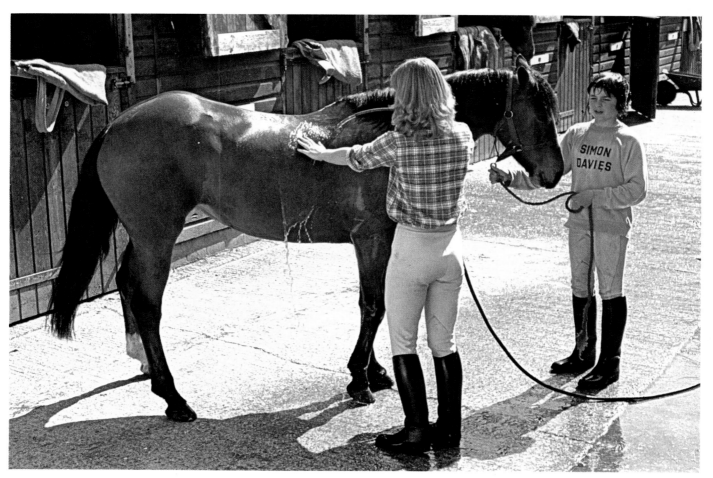

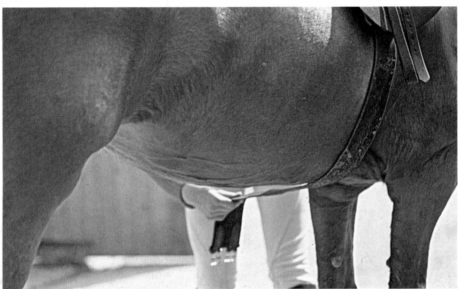

gently with your hands or rub them in case they are cold. If a horse or pony's ears are cold, then he will be cold all over. If they are warm, then the rest of his body will also be warm. Pick out, wash and oil the feet and hooves as before and brush the mane, tail and face in the same way, with the body brush.

In summertime, grass-kept ponies can be groomed more thoroughly since they do not have the same need for the grease in their coats to keep them warm and dry. This thorough grooming is known as 'strapping' and it helps to make the coat shine. The procedure is outlined on page 68.

Tacking up

Once the pony has been groomed, he can be tacked-up ready to receive his rider. The saddle should be put on first, while the pony is still tethered. When you fetch the saddle from the tack room, the stirrup irons should be run up the leathers so that they are resting against the top sides of the saddle, and the girth should be folded over the seat. The easiest and best way to carry a saddle is to rest it over your left arm with the pommel in the crook of your elbow. Support the other end with your right hand and take it to the pony's nearside, standing by his shoulder.

Lift the saddle up on to the pony's back, placing it well forward up on the withers (see diagram, page 94), then slide it gently back into place. This way you ensure that the hairs on the animal's back are not ruffled up the wrong way. The correct position for the saddle is so that the pommel lies directly behind the withers. Go round to the pony's other side (where the girth should be buckled) and take it down from the seat of the saddle. Return to the animal's nearside, pull the girth through under the tummy and buckle it. There is no need to buckle it very tightly at this point and most ponies will, in any event, not allow you to do so since they will breathe out very heavily at the precise moment you pull on the

Standing on the pony's nearside, slide the saddle gently into place, just behind the withers (top). Bring the girth under the pony's tummy (centre) and buckle it firmly (left).

girth straps. Just buckle them on whatever hole you can, then run your fingers down between the pony's skin and the girth to make sure the hairs are lying smoothly and the skin is not wrinkled. By now the pony will probably have had to take another breath and you can therefore tighten the girths a hole or two. Leave the stirrup irons run up the leathers until the rider is ready to mount. That way they will not bang against the pony's side if he moves about or is restless.

Putting on the bridle

If the pony is wanted straight away, put on the bridle too. Hold it in your left hand by the headpiece and stand on the pony's nearside at his head. Untie the headcollar rope but, before removing the headcollar, put the reins of the bridle over the pony's head so that they are looped round his neck. Now remove the headcollar and transfer the top of the bridle to your right hand. Rest this hand on top of the pony's head with the browband and noseband (see page 116) facing forward. Hold the bit in your left hand and, with your fingers, gently feel at the corners of the mouth to encourage the pony to open his mouth. As he does so, slide the bit into his mouth taking care not to bang his teeth. Pull the ears through between the headpieces and the browband so the bridle is in position. Pull the forelock out over the top of the browband.

Buckle the noseband, assuming it is an ordinary cavesson (see page 126), and make sure it lies inside the cheek straps. Then buckle the throatlash. These are sufficiently tight if you can get the width of two fingers between the noseband and the pony's nose and your whole hand between the throat and the throatlash.

The pony is now ready to receive his rider. There are various ways in which you can be of assistance here, according to how the rider intends to get up into the saddle. First of all, check the girths to ensure that they are sufficiently tight for the saddle not to slip round under

Holding the bridle as shown (top), gently open the pony's mouth to take the bit. Pull the ears through the headpiece (centre); buckle the throatlash and noseband (right).

the pony's tummy as soon as any pressure is put on the iron. Then pull the stirrup irons down the leathers.

If the rider is going to mount from the ground, hold the pony still by standing in front of him and holding a rein in each hand immediately behind the bit, while the rider mounts and settles into the saddle. It may be, though, that the rider will want to mount from a mounting block (most stable yards have one of these), in which case lead the pony over to it, so that the mounting block is level with the saddle on the nearside. The rider can then step easily into the saddle.

The other way to assist a rider in mounting is to give him or her a 'leg up'. To do this, hold the reins of the bridle in your left hand, a little way along from the bit, and stand on the pony's nearside. The rider will face the saddle and bend his left leg backward from the knee. Support this leg as firmly as possible with your right hand as he

springs up off the ground from his other foot. You must help to support his weight until he has got his right leg across the saddle.

If the rider you are helping is a comparative beginner in the saddle, ask him to put his left leg forward while you check the girths. Usually the weight of a rider makes it possible to tighten the girths a little more. Adjust the length of the stirrup leathers if he does not know how to do so himself. They are approximately the correct length when the iron just touches the ankle bone if the leather is hanging at right angles to the ground.

Between rides

As the riders leave the yard and the hustle and bustle of ride preparation is over, comparative peace seems to descend over the yard. You may wonder what there is to do now to occupy yourself while the ride is out. Never fear, there is always plenty to be done

between rides, which in most riding schools last for about one hour.

First of all, collect the headcollars which have been discarded and are probably littered around the yard, hanging from posts and dangling from rings. They should be hung up in the tack room until they are needed again. If you feel you have time, this is also a good opportunity to give them a good washing and soaping. Headcollars often get overlooked at general tack cleaning times and it is important to keep them as clean and supple as the rest of a horse's or pony's tack or they will soon rub a sore patch on the animal's face. Now is also the time to clean any tack that is not being used and is due for a clean (see page 126).

Giving the child a leg-up helps her to mount (left). Adjust the length of the stirrup leathers (below) and tighten the girth when the rider is in the saddle (right).

and check to make sure they have not pushed against the fence anywhere and begun to create a weak spot. There should be no loose posts, broken rails or trailing wires. If there are, you may be sure that any pony will seek them out in no time at all and force his way out to even greater freedom beyond. Make a mental note of any weak spots and remember to tell the owner of the stables. In doing your rounds make sure picnickers or passers-by have not thrown in any rubbish that could be harmful. Bottles, drink cans, polythene bags and such like all present a potential hazard that could cause a horse or pony distress or injury.

Another useful thing to do is to clean out the water tank if it has begun to collect a covering of slime and a surface flotilla of fallen leaves. If it is a ball-cock-operated tank, turn off the water at the mains, then bail out all the water in the tank, using a bucket. Do not, of course, dispose of this in a part of the field that is already damp or muddy. Scrub the tank with a scrubbing brush and clean water. Do not use any detergent or soapy liquid, since it will be impossible to remove completely and will contaminate the water when you refill the tank. Turn the water on again but do not go away and leave it or this will be the day that the ball-cock mechanism fails and the tank overflows! Come back when it has had time to refill just to make sure everything is in proper working order.

Things to do

It will help to conserve the grazing and keep it sweeter if you go round the field with a shovel and wheelbarrow removing the droppings each day. Horses are fussy grazers, unlike cattle and sheep, and do not like eating grass that they have contaminated. Take the droppings back to the manure heap.

If it is a time of year when the ponies are being fed, you could make up the feeds while the ride is out, so as to save time later. Most stables will have a list, probably nailed to the feed-room door or wall, stating the quantities of different feedstuffs to give each animal. Follow these instructions carefully and remember to make a note of any foodstuff that is getting in short supply so that you can tell whoever is responsible

Next, tidy the yard. Remove all droppings, using a shovel and wheelbarrow or sack kept for the purpose. Take them straight to the dung heap, which is generally round the back of the stables. Even if it is out of immediate sight, this should be kept neat and tidy and not allowed to straggle, which can easily happen. Sweep the yard thoroughly, using a stiff-bristled broom. If necessary, swill it down with buckets of water. Brush any surplus water away so that there is not a mass of puddles around the yard.

If the ponies were brought in from

Sweeping the yard is one of the essential daily chores and should be done several times a day.

grass and put in the stable, remove any droppings and shake up the bedding, adding to it if necessary. There is no need to muck out the stables thoroughly (see page 68) if a pony has only stood in them for an hour or two.

The time in between rides also provides an opportunity to catch up any ponies not being ridden, give them a perfunctory groom and generally make a fuss of them. Also go round the field

to order some more. Hay nets can be filled, too – these are big string bags, which have a draw string at the top. Open this as wide as possible, then shake out some large wodges of hay and push them into the net. When you have filled the nets to capacity, pull up the draw string and either tie the nets up in the stable or leave them on the hay bales ready to go out to the field. Wash out and refill any water buckets in the stables, so that there is fresh water in each one. Shortly before the ride is due to return, prepare any ponies not currently being ridden that are wanted for the next ride.

While the ride is out is the best time to make sure that the yard, stables, field, tack room and feed room are neat, tidy and in good working order. The more that can be done at this stage to prepare feed, clean tack, fill hay nets and so on, the less there is to do at the end of the day.

If the ride has been away for about an hour, you are likely to find the riders coming back into the yard long before you are through with all the chores you

had planned to do. However, as soon as they return, you must give your attention to the ponies.

Respite for the pony

First of all, help the riders from the saddle. Your job is really no more than to hold the pony still while the rider himself dismounts. If he does not pat and make a fuss of the pony, do so yourself as reward for his hard work.

If the pony is due to go out again straight away on a ride, there is little to be done. You could loosen off the girth a hole or two for the few minutes' respite the pony will have. If he has been brought back into the yard hot and sweating, walk him round until the new rider is ready to mount. If a hot pony is left standing still, he will soon become shivery and may easily catch cold. If he is cool and there is time to tie him up before going out again, remove the bridle and put on the headcollar. Alternatively, you can put the head-collar on over the bridle but on no account tie or secure the pony by the reins. If anything frightens him, he will

instantly pull back and you may find yourself paying for a broken bridle, which is not a cheap item.

If the pony is not wanted for an hour or so, he can meanwhile be put in the stable, with the bridle and saddle removed, providing he is dry. If he is wet, either from rain or sweat, he should not be put in the stable unless he is covered with dry straw and a sack (see page 13). When wet, he is better off outside, either being walked gently around if he is hot, or tethered quietly if he is wet from rain. Remove or cover the saddle if it is raining so that it does not become sodden. That would be uncomfortable for the next rider and would harm the leather.

Sooner or later, of course, the day's rides will be finished and the ponies can be turned out in the field again. Remove the saddle and bridle, loop the reins over your left arm and run the stirrup irons up the leathers on both

Remove the last dregs of water from the tank with a sponge before scrubbing it and refilling.

sides of the saddle. Undo the girth from the nearside, then gently pull the saddle over the pony's back towards you. As the girth slides across the pony's back, take hold of it and put it across the seat of the saddle. The side that was against the pony should rest against the saddle so as to prevent the seat getting scratched from any bits of hard mud that may have splashed on to the girth during the ride. Put the saddle either across a fence (if it is not likely to be knocked off) or rest it on the ground in a place where it is not likely to be kicked or tripped over by grooms or ponies. If you stand a saddle on the ground (and this is only ever a temporary measure), it should stand on its pommel.

Loop the reins around the pony's neck and unbuckle the throatlash and noseband. Holding the bridle by the headpiece, slip it forward off the pony's head. Let him drop the bit gently from his mouth. Do not pull it out so that you bang the animal's teeth. Put on the headcollar while the reins are still looped round the pony's neck, so that you have hold of him should he try to move away from you.

Turning out routine

If the pony has had a long day, take a handful of clean straw and rub him briskly on the saddle mark to help dry off the sweat and to restore the circulation to these areas. Rub the ears too, either with straw or with your hands. If it is a cold winter's day, you could offer the pony a bucket of tepid water, but do not be perturbed if he does not want to drink. He will do so in the field in his own good time and the cold water there is unlikely to cause him any harm.

Pick out the feet again, in case any stones have become lodged during the rides. Give the animal a quick look over for any injury he may have sustained. Run your hands down his legs to feel for cuts, bumps or scratches and treat them as described in Chapter five.

As with catching a pony, there is a

To turn a pony out in the field, lead him quietly through the gate, taking care not to let the others out (top). Shut the gate behind you, then remove the headcollar. Pat him for his hard work (centre) then let him join his fieldmates (right).

As a temporary measure saddles should be left across a fence or stood on their pommel.

right and wrong way of turning him out in the field. Many ponies become difficult to catch because not enough thought has been given to the way they are turned out. Lead your pony quietly to the field and through the gate, shutting it behind you. Walk him a short distance into the field, then turn him round to face the gate. This is a precaution. If the pony whips round as soon as you release it, kicking up his heels in exhilaration at his freedom, you will have a better chance of making a quick retreat out of the field than you would if the pony were between you and the gate. Stand still for a minute or two, hold the pony and make a fuss of him and perhaps give him a small titbit

to let him know that his hard work has been appreciated. Unbuckle and remove the halter, pat the pony again and walk out of the field at once. It is a good idea to leave the pony before he moves. On no account encourage him to gallop off across the field by waving your arms and slapping him on the rump with your hand or the headcollar rope. Horses and ponies are creatures of habit and will soon learn to be excitable when turned out, if made to charge off into the distance.

If more ponies are to be turned out in the field at the same time, arrange with the other helpers to do so at about five-minute intervals. Turn one out and then return to the yard to collect the next. If you turn out more than one pony at a time, there is a great chance that they will incite one another to dash for freedom across the field.

After a day of rides, the first thing most ponies will do when turned out is to roll, usually in the muddiest or dirtiest corner of the field they can find. This actually helps to dry them off if they are wet from sweat, or to warm them up if they are a little chilled. After a good shake, they generally make for the water tank and take a long drink. It is important that a horse or pony drinks *before* having a feed rather than after it, when the feed would be washed straight through the stomach. Do not put any feeds out in the field until about fifteen minutes after turning out the ponies.

When turning out and feeding routine are complete, the yard and feed room have to be swept and tidied, tack has to be cleaned (see page 126) and everything made ready for the next day. By the time you have finished you will have every right to feel tired!

2 Riding and jumping

The horse is among the oldest forms of transport. For countless generations, the horse's role was confined to helping man in his daily life and toil. It is only in the last few decades that riding has become a leisure activity available to most people. The attractions of riding are obvious. It can be enjoyed by both young and old, in either urban or rural areas. It can be pursued to different levels, from an hour or two's gentle hack at the weekend to the highest points of competition in show jumping, racing or eventing.

In effect, riding offers greater variety than most other sports. There are so many different fields of horsemanship – polo, eventing, trekking, hunting, show jumping, racing, showing and dressage, to name just some. Yet all of these begin with the same basic groundwork. Whichever path a rider decides to pursue, he must first learn to sit correctly and to control a horse.

Riding has its dangers, too. Just as a motor car would be a menace in the hands of someone who did not know how to drive, so a highly-strung horse ridden by a beginner could wreak havoc. Horses must be properly trained and riders must be properly taught, or the combination can be lethal. It is for this reason, above all, that the choice of riding school is very important.

The right approach

From the point of view of the novice, most riding schools may be broadly divided into two categories: those that sit you on a sluggish horse, or pony, attached to a leading rein and haul you along on a ride with little or no explanation of what you should or should not be doing; and those that give serious instruction, often at first in an indoor manege or marked-out school area in a field. The latter is obviously preferable. An hour alone with a good instructor is worth several hours of being towed aimlessly and uncomfortably along roads or tracks.

Hacking with friends through fields and woodlands is one of the great joys of being able to ride.

A small group of novice riders receive instruction in a specially constructed covered school.

If you are going to learn to ride at the school where you have been helping with the daily routine, you will have had a chance to get to know the horses and ponies too. Good horsemanship depends very much on trust and the relationship established between horse and rider. You will have a greater understanding of these things if you spend some time with the animal. Take the trouble to observe its behaviour and its reactions, before you mount.

Horses and ponies are sensitive, if not over-intelligent, animals. If you are nervous and hesitant, the horse is likely to be so too. He will react to your mood rather than understand your nervousness. Similarly, if you are calm, gentle and sympathetic in your handling of the horse, the chances are that he will respond in the same way.

Remember, when you start learning to ride, that it takes time to become a competent horseman or horsewoman. No-one becomes expert at anything new overnight, so be prepared to work hard at it. Above all, never despair.

The more thoroughly you learn and practise the basic aspects of horsemanship, that is, developing a well-balanced seat and good sympathetic hands which operate independently from the rest of your movements, the more automatic such action will become. Time and effort spent now, however far away the goal may seem, will pay dividends before too long.

Although there is no need at this stage to kit yourself out with a vast wardrobe of immaculately tailored, expensive riding clothes, some items are essential. Most important of these is a hard hat, which should always be worn when riding. The reinforced crown of the conventional velvet-covered riding hat protects the rider's head from both falls and the possibility of being knocked out by overhanging branches. If you do happen to have a fall on your head, have the riding hat checked immediately after. The crown may be damaged so that it no longer offers the proper protection.

Probably the next most important item of clothing is footwear. Soft shoes, shoes with buckles, separate soles or no heel should not be worn. It is best to buy a pair of proper riding boots, either short jodhpur boots or knee-length riding boots. Specially made rubber riding boots are available now. They are considerably cheaper than leather ones but are perfectly satisfactory for most riders. Never ride in Wellington boots. They tend either to slip on the stirrup iron or get jammed in it.

A pair of strong, well-fitting jeans may be worn, but again it is much better to invest in a pair of jodhpurs or breeches. They are more comfortable and look smarter. What you wear above the waist will generally depend on the weather; a shirt, jumper and anorak (if necessary) will suffice. If you wish to be more 'correct', you should wear a specially tailored riding jacket. These are usually made of some sort of tweed for ordinary hacking.

The only other item to consider is a pair of gloves. Gloves are not necessary on warm, dry days, but should be worn if it is raining as it is hard to grip wet reins with bare hands. Riding gloves are made of string which does not slip.

This is the correct way for the stirrup leather to face when your foot is in the iron.

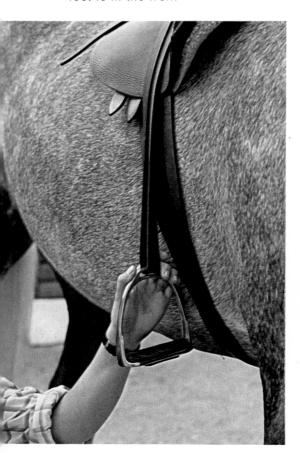

They are also surprisingly warm, though you can buy wool-lined gloves for extra warmth.

Now you are ready to learn to mount your horse or pony. Initially, someone will of course be there to assist you and to hold the animal still but this is something you must learn to do yourself as you make further progress.

Mounting

Before preparing to mount, check that the girths are tight and pull the stirrup irons down the leathers on either side. You can check to see if the leathers are approximately the correct length by placing your hand at the top and stretching the leather out under your arm. The bottom of the iron should reach your armpit.

Face the animal's tail and stand by its shoulder on the 'nearside' (left side). Taking up the reins in your left hand, separate them with your middle two fingers and put the surplus rein over to the 'offside' (right side) of the neck. You should hold the reins tightly enough to prevent your horse or pony from moving. Get into the habit of keeping the offside, or right, rein fractionally

The correct seat and position in the saddle is supremely important.

Take care not to brush the pony's back as you mount. Lower yourself gently into the saddle (right).

---

shorter so that if the pony does try to move, his head will turn away from you rather than towards you.

Take hold of the stirrup leather in your right hand and twist it towards you so that the upper surface of the leather is facing you. Put your left foot in the iron, pointing the toe downwards so as not to dig into the animal's side.

Take hold of a good strand of mane in your left hand, together with the reins, turn towards the pony's side and put your right hand either on the pommel or across the waist of the saddle just behind the pommel. Spring lightly up from the ground off your right foot and swing your right leg across the saddle, trying not to brush the pony's back as you do so. At the same time, move your right hand forward and allow yourself to sink into the saddle. There is a temptation when mounting to haul yourself up by holding on to the back of the saddle. Try to resist this. Not only are you likely to pull the saddle over the back towards you, but you can also twist and deform the foundation or framework of the saddle in time.

A correct seat

Once seated in the saddle, put your right foot quietly into the iron so that the surface of the leather that normally rests against the saddle faces forward. The left leather will already be like this if you followed the instructions given earlier. Positioned in this way, the leather lies flat against your leg and the edge does not dig into you.

It is unlikely that you will feel very comfortable even when you first find yourself astride your horse or pony. The correct position in the saddle is quite different from your normal posture, either when standing up or sitting in a chair. You will be tempted to sit back on your seat, so that your legs are pushed forward and your shoulders are rounded – all of which could not be more wrong!

Establishing the correct seat and position in the saddle is among the most important aspects of learning to ride, for your seat will affect the pony's

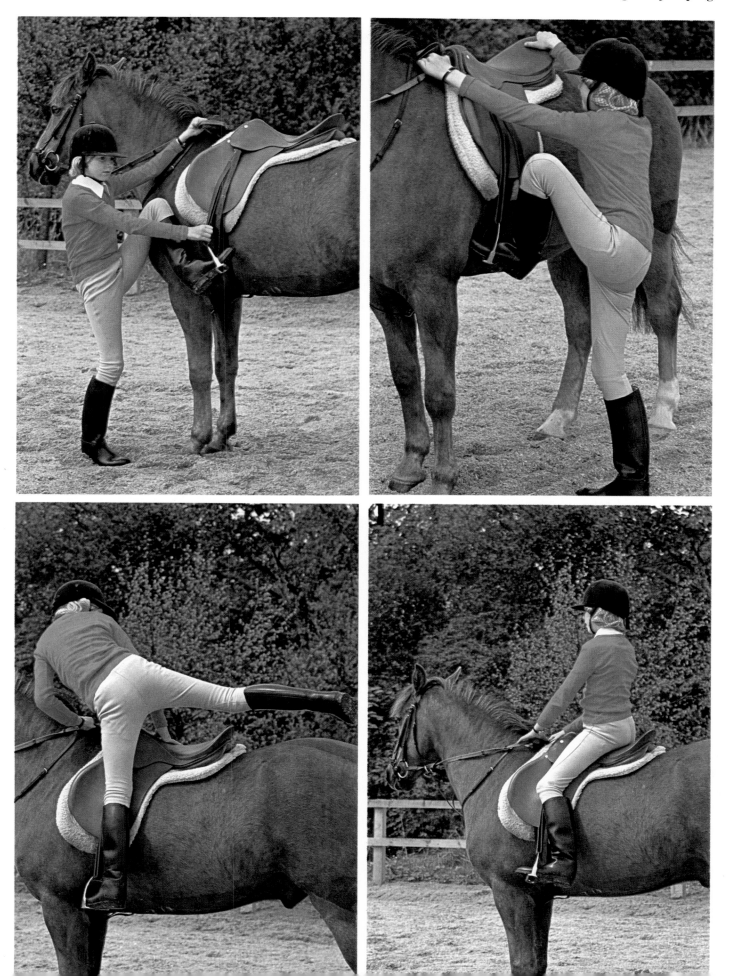

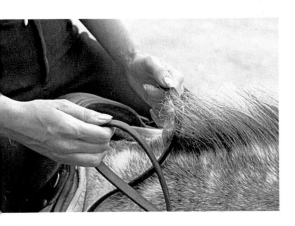

The reins pass between third and fourth fingers. Your thumbs rest on top of the reins, facing forwards.

movement and performance as well as your security and efficiency as a rider. Consider it from the pony's point of view. He has a natural centre of gravity which alters according to how fast he is moving and whether he is turning or going up or down hill. Unencumbered by a rider, he can adapt to conditions accordingly; but a wrongly positioned rider or one that does not adjust his weight to the pony's shifting centre of gravity will severely impede the animal's movement. Your aim, therefore, is to develop a seat that is secure, yet supple and sufficiently balanced to allow you to remain in the saddle in harmony with the pony's movement and pace, while offering him the minimum resistance or discomfort.

First of all you must, of course, learn to adopt the correct position while the pony is standing still. The point of balance that corresponds to the pony's centre of gravity is the lowest part of his back, just behind the withers. This should govern the position of the saddle. For a correctly positioned saddle the lowest part is the right place for the rider to sit.

The proper way to sit in the saddle is as if you were standing on the ground with your knees apart and bent at an angle of approximately 45 degrees to the ground. Your hips should be supple and your back straight so that there is an imaginary straight line running from your heels up through your hips to your shoulders. You should sit on your seat bones rather than your buttocks – even though the latter may be better padded and more comfortable! Push your hips forward and turn your thighs inwards so that the flat part of them rests against the saddle. Your knees should be bent, but relaxed and supple, and rest against the sides of the saddle.

The majority of a rider's body weight is supported by the seat bones, thighs and knees, *not* by the feet resting in the stirrup. However, the correct position in the saddle is maintained by balance, not grip. For this reason your thighs and knees should just rest against the saddle. Do not attempt to grip the sides of the saddle. If you do you will find that you stiffen your knees and thighs

The natural aids, hands, legs and body, and the artificial aids, whip, spurs and martingale, are shown.

An experienced showjumper demonstrates the best use both of the natural aids, and of the artificial aids to riding.

and, instead of sitting deep into the saddle, you will, in no time, have pushed yourself out of it so that you are perching on top.

Allow the lower part of your legs, from the knees, to drop down naturally so that the stirrup leathers hang at right angles to the ground. The balls of your feet should rest on the stirrup irons and your ankles should be relaxed, so that your heels are lower than your toes. The inside of your calf rests against the saddle and you should ensure that you exert no conscious grip whatsoever.

The position of your upper body is of paramount importance, too. Pushing your hips forward will have the effect of straightening your back and this is what you are aiming for – a straight back with no rounding of the shoulders. Your head is held high and looks straight ahead between the pony's ears. In spite of such uprightness, your upper body should also be relaxed and supple, ready to adjust and move with the pony's movement.

Your arms hang naturally in a straight line down to your elbows, which are held neatly against your sides. There should be a straight line running from the bit up the reins and through your hands and arms to your elbows. This is very important.

Finally, we consider the position of the hands and how to hold the reins. Although this may sound as if it is the first thing you should know, it is actually of secondary importance to establishing your position in the saddle. It is impossible to develop sympathetic hands, able to operate independently from the rest of your movements, unless you have first developed a secure, balanced seat.

The reins are held one in each hand. They should pass upwards through your hands between your third and little finger and are held against your index finger with your thumb. Your thumbs should be the highest point of your hands and should point forwards. In order to have that straight line

running through from the reins to your elbows, you must hold your hands just above the pony's withers about 10 cm (4 in) apart. Keep your wrists supple, but not too rounded or your hands and grip on the reins will become stiff. There is no need to grasp the reins tightly and you *must* resist all temptation to hang on to them or use them as a lever. Instead they should be allowed to move with the pony's head so as gently to maintain a constant, steady contact.

Keeping your balance

To begin with, you will probably find sitting in the saddle fairly uncomfortable. You are likely to tire quickly, too, because you are using muscles that are usually inactive. Do not, however, alter your position to one that feels more comfortable. If you allow yourself to get into bad habits now, you will find them almost impossible to break.

Some simple exercises at this stage can both help to relax you and improve your balance. They will assist you in co-ordinating the movements of your legs, arms and body and in maintaining better balance in the saddle. Practise these exercises while somebody is holding the pony's head to keep him still. Later on you can do them at a walk, trot, and even a canter, but obviously this is very much in the future! All of the exercises given below will both help to improve your balance and make you feel more confident and secure in the saddle.

Keeping the lower part of your body still and correctly positioned, hold the reins in one hand and lean forward to touch the animal's ears with the other hand. Sit up straight again, lean down and touch your toes and, finally, lean back and touch the pony's tail. Transfer the reins to the other hand and repeat the exercise. Try to make the whole of this exercise one continuous, flowing movement, but keep your seat and legs quite still.

Again, keeping the lower part of your body still and in the correct position, hold the reins in the left hand and lean

Exercises help to supple and balance you. Make sure someone holds the pony if the exercise entails you letting go of the reins.

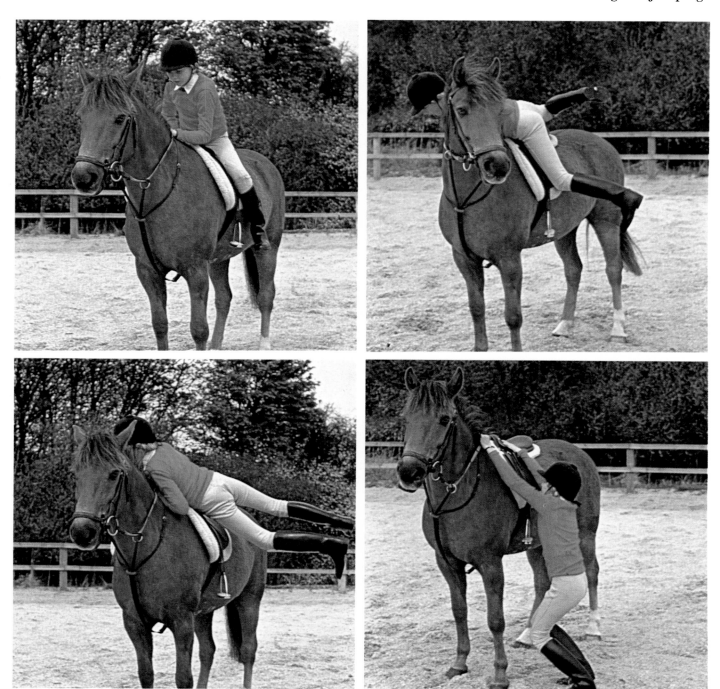

Remember to take both feet out of the irons before dismounting. Bend your knees as you land on the ground so as not to jar yourself.

over and touch the left toe with your right hand. Return to a normal sitting position and repeat the exercise on the other side.

Sit in the correct position and hold the reins with one hand. Keeping the other arm straight, move it in a wide circle from your shoulder. Move only one arm, not the rest of your upper body. Repeat with the other arm.

Take both feet out of the stirrup irons, then circle your feet from the ankles. first to the right and then to the left. This is useful for suppling your ankles.

It is *essential* that someone holds the pony while you do the next two exercises. Drop the reins altogether and fold your arms. Then, keeping the lower part of your body still, lean right forward until your head almost touches the pony's neck. Sit up straight again and lean back until your head is almost

touching his back. Make sure that your legs stay in the correct position all the time.

Take both feet out of the stirrup irons and drop the reins on the pony's neck. Put your left leg over the front of the saddle so that you are sitting sideways on the pony's back. Put your right leg over his back so you are sitting facing the tail. Then bring your left leg over his back so you are facing to the left. Finally, take your right leg back over the front of the saddle so that you are correctly positioned again. Do the exer-

cise first to the left and then to the right, again trying to make it one continuous movement rather than stopping at each point, so that the action is smooth.

The natural aids

Once established in the saddle, you will, of course, need to know how to communicate your wishes to your pony. The conventional signals, or corresponding means of giving them, are known as *aids*. They fall into two groups: natural aids, those given with the hands, legs, body and, to some extent, the voice; and artificial aids, which involve the use of whips, spurs and ancillary items of tack such as martingales. The artificial aids should only be used by horsemen and horsewomen who know how to use them properly and effectively.

There are two very important points about aids that should be remembered at all times. They should always be used in conjunction with one another and in a manner so discreet that the onlooker sees no movement from the rider. A signal from the legs is always accompanied by a corresponding complementary signal from the hands and body. Horses and ponies are trained to understand such signals and will respond accordingly, provided the correct aid has been given.

In so far as it is possible to consider the natural aids individually, the legs in effect create forward movement in the pony. They are used to maintain the so-called impulsion and also to guide and control the pony's hindquarters, which are the source of power for his motion. The weight of the body as it shifts in the saddle can serve to alter both the balance and direction of the pony. The hands control the direction and forehand (see diagram, page 94) as well as allowing faster movement and lengthening of the stride, or alternatively checking the pace and shortening the stride. The voice is used mainly in the training of a young horse and does not generally assume a very important role, particularly in a novice rider. It can, of course, be used to calm and soothe a

---

Walking in a dead straight line is considerably more difficult than it sounds. Try this by moving from one fixed point to another.

nervous pony or as a means of attracting his attention.

Just as it is important to apply the aids in conjunction with one another, so it follows that they should never contradict one another. If, for example, you use your legs to suggest forward movement, you must allow the pony to obey you by relaxing your hold accordingly. When you are using your hands to check your pony's pace, do not pull on the reins. There are many reasons for this, not least of which is that it will cause the pony acute pain and eventually make him hard-mouthed. A horse's or pony's reaction if he receives a dead pull on his mouth will be to pull back in an effort to stop the pressure. If you continue pulling, so will he, which is how horses and ponies that are confirmed 'pullers' develop.

As your hands control the energy created by the pony's legs, you should always push him forward into the bit, whatever command you are going to give. Even if you want him to stop, he must first be pushed forward so that he meets with resistance from your hand and stops with his hindquarters well beneath him, instead of with his hind legs straggling out behind him. For this reason, too, the aids from your legs and body, which push the pony forward, should always be given fractionally before the corresponding signal from your hands.

Dismounting

Before considering the various paces of the pony, let us look at how to dismount. There are a number of ways of doing this, but really only one that should be practised at this stage.

Having brought the pony to a halt, take both feet out of the stirrup irons and transfer the reins to your left hand. Place your right hand on the pony's shoulder or along his neck and lean forward. Swing your right leg up behind you, over the back of the saddle, and jump down to the ground landing on both feet. Remember to 'give' with your knees and ankles, so you do not land with a jarring thud. After dismounting, you can run the stirrup irons up the leathers and either slacken the girth or take the saddle off altogether, depending upon your immediate intentions for you and your pony.

Always take the reins over the animal's head to lead him. You have greater control than if they are still looped around his neck. And remember, too, to pat and make a fuss of him at the end of a lesson, however stiff and aching your muscles may feel as a result of your ride! He surely deserves it.

The walk

The first movement of the pony that you are likely to experience is the walk. This is a marching pace in four-time in which each leg leaves and strikes the ground individually, so that you hear four distinct hoof beats. A good walk is evenly balanced. The time intervals between each foot leaving and returning to the ground are regular. Providing the rider maintains a gentle, but constant feel on the reins the pony's head will be held fairly high and will swing up and down with the rhythm of the movement.

To give the pony the signal, or aid, to move into a walk from a stationary position, sit deep into the saddle, exerting pressure with your seat bones, and gently close your legs against his sides. Immediately you feel him respond, flex your wrists slightly so that your hands give and you allow your mount to move forward.

Your position in the saddle at the walk does not fundamentally change. Allow your upper body to sway very slightly with the movement, letting your hips swing with the swing of the pony's hips. Your hands, too, must continually give with the pony's head movement, although they should not actually move. A little 'elasticity' in your wrists is all that is needed.

You will very soon get used to the feel of the walk and may find its even rhythm makes you feel more comfortable in the saddle than you did at a halt. However, it is important not just to sit there so complacently and comfortably that the pony begins to dawdle and become lazy. At this point, the pace will lack any impulsion because you have ceased to create any. You must therefore keep pressing the pony forward gently, by maintaining the pressure from your seat bones and legs as necessary.

Resist any temptation to give leg aids involving kicking the pony in the sides.

The fact that you are almost sure to have seen other riders do so in no way makes it correct! A pony reacts sharply to any quick or sudden movement and a kick in the sides is likely to make a well-trained animal leap forwards. The result would almost certainly be to unseat you, if not right out of the saddle, at least enough to make you lose your carefully practised position and probably deliver a sharp tug on the reins in your effort to maintain your balance. It is equally as bad to flap your legs repeatedly against the pony's sides. This is not only quite ineffective, it also results in these areas becoming deadened and insensitive, so that the pony eventually no longer responds to normal leg aids.

Controlling direction

As the walk is the easiest pace for the novice rider, it is a good one for practising simple turns and moving in perfectly straight lines. The latter is actually more difficult to do than you may think and yet it is very helpful in teaching you how to control a pony's

direction. So once you have got used to the feel of the walking pace and are able to maintain sufficient impulsion to give a constant steady walk, steer your pony in a straight line from one point to another marked point. Position the marker so that it is visible as you look between the pony's ears. Keep looking directly at it as you walk towards it, holding your head high. This is important, for if you look down you will slouch forward and lose your upright posture.

When the rider wants the pony to turn to the left or right, he must point him in that direction by exerting slight pressure on the reins. The forehand leads the body round the corner, but the energy and propulsion must still come from the hindquarters. Before delivering the aids for a turn, you should make sure your pony is attentive and ready to obey you, at the same time letting him know you are about to give some directional instruction. To do this, just sit a little deeper in the saddle and close your legs against his sides. Increase your feel on the reins very slightly, but not enough to bring the

At a sitting trot, sit deep in the saddle and relax, keeping your back straight and your legs still.

pony back to a halt. A well-trained pony should respond to such light, gentle aids and prepare himself to receive your next instruction.

Now suppose you wish to turn to the right. Close your right leg on the girth and then your left leg just behind it. Exert very slight pressure on the right rein, at the same time yielding slightly with the left rein. Let us examine the effects of these aids. By exerting pressure on the girth with your right leg, at the same time maintaining and encouraging the forward movement, you indicate that you want the pony to bend round this point. In so doing however, the natural tendency would be for the animal's hindquarters to swing out to the left, but the pressure from your left leg prevents this and keeps his hind feet following in the same tracks as the forefeet. Pressure on the right rein bends and leads the forehand in that direction, while yielding

At a rising trot, rise very gently from the hips in time with the trotting rhythm.

with the left hand allows this movement to take place.

When making a turn, the pony's body should bend in an even arc. In other words, the head and neck should not be bent at an angle to the rest of the body, neither should the pace alter throughout the turn. As soon as the turn is completed, stop applying the aids and resume your normal position.

When you want the pony to come to a halt, you must again prepare him for being given a new instruction. Sit deep into the saddle, close your legs and offer gentle resistance with your hands. Allow the weight of your body to shift back very slightly at the same time as you increase the feel on the reins. What you are doing is pushing the pony forward up to the bit, but then resisting any further forward movement by the pressure of your hands on the reins. The pony should halt squarely with its legs tucked well beneath it. The minute he

does so, relax the pressure of your hands, lengthen the reins and sit quietly.

If you exert pressure on the reins to stop the pony without giving any accompanying aids from your legs and body, you are not collecting your pony together to prepare him for a halt. If he does come to a stop at such a crude instruction, it will be with his legs askew instead of positioned squarely beneath him, and his head up in the air trying to evade the unpleasant pressure of the bit in his mouth.

The trot

The pace that follows on from the walk, that is, the trot, is one of the most difficult for the new rider to master. It is a pace in two-time, in which the pony moves opposite diagonal legs, off-fore and near-hind together and near-fore and off-hind together. It is a springy pace, since the pony springs from one pair of diagonals to the other, an action that tends to throw the rider around in the saddle, at least until he or she has become used to the motion. For this

reason, there is little point in attempting the trot until you have really consolidated your position and developed a balanced and secure seat at the walk.

There are two ways of riding at the trot: either by rising out of the saddle at each alternate stride or by maintaining permanent contact with the saddle. The first of these is known as the rising, or posting, trot; the second, the sitting trot. The rising trot is actually less tiring for both pony and rider, although you may find this hard to believe when you are being bumped about in the saddle and probably only managing to rise once every six strides at best! At first, you will most certainly be bumped around in the saddle. If you feel insecure, hold on to a lock of mane or the pommel and just try to relax. Whatever you do, do not use the reins to steady yourself.

Listen to the beat of the pony's hooves at a trot. You will hear a definite 'one-two', 'one-two'. This corresponds to the up-down action of the rising trot. As you rise, your body should be inclined slightly forward (but

only very slightly). Your thigh, knee and lower leg remain in the same position. Try to let the movement of the horse push your body up, your knees acting as hinges. You should not rise consciously. If you do, you are likely to develop a stiff, hollow back from the effort and your stomach will be pushed forward. At the same time you may find you are gripping like mad with your knees and thighs, upsetting your balance and making the rest of your body stiff. In no time at all, you will be relying on your hands to steady yourself and restore your balance.

Make sure you are keeping your hands still as you try to master the rising action. There is quite a temptation to bob them up and down with the movement of your body but, as ever, they should act quite independently.

Smoothness at a sitting trot is, if anything, even harder to achieve. Although your aim is now to sit deep into the saddle, maintaining permanent contact, with your legs in their normal position, you are still going to be bumped around at first. In fact, you may find it easier to practise a sitting trot with your feet out of the stirrup irons. This eliminates any tendency to support your weight on the stirrups by pressing on them, which has the effect of making you lose your balance rather than keeping it. Again, it is a good idea to steady yourself by taking hold of a lock of mane or the pommel and so spare the pony's mouth. This will also help you to stay in the right place in the saddle.

Only attempt a sitting trot for a few strides at a time and preferably with the horse moving at a slow trot, for it will be very tiring. If you allow yourself to get too tired so that the muscles are exhausted, you will have no hope of being able to master either the sitting or rising trot.

Aids for moving from a walk to a trot are much the same as those for moving from a halt to a walk, although, again, make sure your pony is paying attention and is ready to respond to any signal you give him. Then close your

There should be no jerky movement from pony or rider as they effect a transition from walk to trot, as shown in these pictures.

legs firmly behind the girth and yield with your hands. It is a good idea to shorten the reins a fraction to begin with as the head carriage at a trot is higher than it is at a walk. Thus the reins automatically become a little slacker. Relax the pressure from your legs as soon as the pony breaks into a trot.

Aids for turning left and right at the trot are the same as for the walk, although it is preferable to master the rising and sitting movements before trying to give such aids. You will find it hard enough even to think about them, let alone actually give them, when being bumped around in the saddle. Always give the aids for a turn from a sitting, rather than a rising, trot.

To slow back to a walk from a trot, sit deep into the saddle, again pushing the pony forward into the bit, and resist gently with your hands. If you want to bring him back to a halt, relax the aids while he walks a few strides, then re-apply them to ask him to stop.

The canter

After the trot comes the canter, which is a pace that can sometimes seem like a blessed relief to a rider who has been thrown about endlessly at a trot! In fact, the canter should not be attempted until both the rising and sitting trot have been properly mastered. Smooth though the pace can be, a novice rider will still experience a fair amount of bumping around in the saddle.

The canter is a pace in three-time, so that each complete stride has three hoof beats followed by a moment of suspension. The sequence of the legs is either near-hind, followed by off-hind and near-fore moving together, and finally off-fore; or off-hind, followed by near-hind and off-fore, and then near-fore. This sequence is known as a 'united canter'. If it is broken, which can happen, the horse is said to be 'cantering disunited'.

The aim of the rider at the canter is to sit deep into the saddle, allowing his body to move in perfect harmony with the rocking action of the stride. The

When making a turn, remember to sit squarely in the saddle. Do not let your inside shoulder 'collapse'.

best way to achieve this is to relax, although that does not mean to slouch, for it is still essential to sit upright with your shoulders well back. Your hips and loins should be relaxed; if you stiffen them you will begin to bump up and down in the saddle. Keep your knees particularly supple at the canter so that the lower part of your legs remain still. There is sometimes a tendency to let them move backwards, which lessens your control and upsets both your balance and position. The other tendency, conversely, is to lean back in the saddle, pushing your lower

---

LEFT: when cantering in a circle, keep the pony on the perimeter. Do not let him fall into the middle.

BELOW: To make the transition from trot to canter, make sure the pony is trotting forward freely and is ready to obey your commands.

legs forward, which puts your weight in quite the wrong place for the movement of the pony.

The pony's head at a canter swings forward and backward to a marked degree with the movement. It is essential that your hands do not interfere with this movement, so you must really keep your wrists very supple and relaxed. Again, this does not mean consciously moving your hands, just allowing them to rock with the rhythm.

Aids for a canter vary slightly depending which leg you want to be the lead. When cantering in a circle, the inner fore leg should appear to be leading (although it is actually the final stage of the canter stride). Thus, if cantering a circle to the right, the first breakdown sequence of legs given on page 35 for a canter would be correct. When moving in a straight line, it does not matter greatly which leg leads, but it is always a good idea to decide which

leg you want to lead and to give the aids accordingly.

It is easiest to ask a pony to canter out of a turn or a corner. First ensure that your pony is moving forwards at a balanced and collected, but lively, trot. Sit well down into the saddle and make sure he is attentive. Apply pressure on the girth with the inside leg, that is, the one on the inside of the turn or bend, and behind the girth with the outside leg. Lean very slightly to the inside, maintaining the pressure with your seat, and at the same time incline the pony's head, too, slightly towards the inside of the bend. He should then strike off with the inside leg leading. As he does, cease the pressure from your legs and let your hands give with the movement. Sit upright in the saddle ready to rock with the motion.

Aids for slowing down from a canter are the same as for slowing down from a trot to a walk except, if anything, you

need to brace your back muscles a little more, thus pushing your seat a fraction further forward. Practise transitions from a trot to a canter and back to a trot. They are the hardest to accomplish really smoothly. Remember, if you want to slow down from a canter to a halt, to allow the horse to move forward for a few strides at the trot and walk. Keep all transitions smooth and as gradual as possible.

Exercises on the move

As you become more at home in the saddle and accustomed to the different paces of the pony, you can try doing some of the exercises outlined on pages 28–31 at a walk, trot and canter. Be sensible about this. Obviously you should not do the exercise where you turn completely round in the saddle whilst the pony is moving. And if you do the leaning forwards and backwards exercise on the move it should only be

Taking your knees and legs forward, away from the saddle, makes you sit on your seat bones.

at a walk with someone leading the horse. The others, however, will help to improve your balance still further and should make your seat more secure in the saddle. The exercises will serve to increase your confidence as a horseman or horsewoman for, the better you feel in the saddle and the more 'at one' with your mount, the better you will enjoy your riding.

The other great value of breaking off from concentrated riding at the various paces to do some exercises is that it helps you to take your mind off how to ride, how you are sitting in the saddle, the way you are holding the reins, and so on. Your aim is to become a more relaxed and instinctive rider, so that all your movements and reactions are made subconsciously and come as second nature to you. This will only happen when you stop thinking hard about what you are doing. Exercises will help divert your attention as you will have to concentrate on how to do them. When you resume a natural position in the saddle after the exercises, it should somehow seem easier.

If you can do the exercises while an instructor 'lunges' your mount, so much the better. You then do not have to worry at all about controlling the pony, so that you can knot the reins around his neck and forget about them. This of course eliminates any possibility of using them to hang on to during some of the more unsettling exercises.

If doing exercises in a school and there is a wall or fence on one side of you, do all those that require a sideward bend or movement of the body away from the wall or fence. For example, when doing the exercise of bending down and touching your toes, lean forward and touch the inside toe. If you lean over and touch the toe nearer the wall, should anything suddenly frighten your pony and make him jump, you could fall off between him and the wall, which could be dangerous.

There are one or two slightly more advanced exercises you could add to your repertoire now that you are becoming a little more experienced. Try sitting on your seat bones and lifting your legs upward in front of you, keep-

ing them straight, so that they are parallel with the pony's withers. Hold the pommel with one hand and be very careful not to jerk the reins if you are not on the lunge. You can do this at a walk, trot and even a canter if you feel sufficiently secure. It is very good for helping your balance as the only contact you have with the saddle is your seat and there is no possible area of grip.

Another exercise to try is to take your legs away from the saddle and, keeping them straight, rotate each in turn from the hips. Rotate the right leg to the right, or clockwise, and the left leg anticlockwise. Then let them resume their proper position. This exercise helps to develop and flatten your thigh muscles and you will probably find them aching to prove it!

Work through all the exercises, repeating each movement two or three times. In between each one, re-establish a correct position for a few strides so that you begin each exercise from the proper basis. If you have been thrown out of position and immediately go on to another exercise, not only will you

probably not do it correctly, but you are that much more likely to lose your balance. It is very important to make sure your legs are in the right position when doing exercises that mainly affect the upper part of your body. The temptation is often to increase your grip so that your legs move too far forward or back.

Also, do not do the exercises for too long a period at a time. They are generally designed to stretch or work some particular muscles and you should feel these aching afterwards. If not, you have not done the exercise properly! But do not continue to the point where you are over-working muscles that are out of condition. They will just become ineffective.

Changing the diagonal

The two paces that require a little more thought and effort as you begin to relax in the saddle are the trot and the canter.

You will remember that the trot is a two-time pace in which opposite diagonal pairs of legs move in unison. Thus,

at the rising trot, you rise as either the left or the right leg goes forward. If you rise as the right leg goes forward you are rising on the right diagonal; if you rise as the left leg goes forward you are rising on the left diagonal. In the early days of your trotting, obviously you are too busy trying to rise in time with the movement to work out which leg is moving forward as you rise. However, it is important for, unless you get into the habit of changing the diagonal when trotting, you will soon find it far more comfortable to ride on one diagonal than the other. The effect of this, besides making your riding lop-sided, is to place additional strain on the pony as more stress is repeatedly put on the muscles of one side. Soon his trot will become asymmetrical and stiff in an effort to counteract this extra strain.

When riding in a circle you should get into the habit of riding on the outside diagonal, that is, rising as the

As you get more experienced, try various exercises when your pony is walking or trotting forwards.

leg on the outside of the circle moves forward. This helps to relieve the muscles on that side, which are having to work harder than those on the inside since the outside legs have to cover fractionally more ground. When you change the rein across the school, you should also change the diagonal – which for a novice is more easily said than done! The way to do it, however, is to sit for one stride or bounce and resume your rising on the next stride, when previously you would have been coming back into the saddle. Thus, if the movement is up-down, up-down, to change the diagonal it should be up-down, down-up. You will find, to begin with, you nearly always bounce for two strides, so that you return to the same diagonal. Persevere and it will come.

When going for a leisurely hack do not forget to change the diagonal from time to time. Because you are not at 'school', in the same way as when you ride in the manege, you tend to forget about such things and allow yourself to relax rather more. If you do, however, you are likely to develop a lop-sided trotting action in both you and your pony.

Work at the canter following the same principle. When riding in a circle, ensure that your pony canters with the correct (inner) leg leading; when out for a hack, change the lead leg from time to time so that you and your mount do not become too used to cantering with the same leg leading all the time. The temptation when out for a hack will, after all, be to push him forward into a canter without thinking about which leg should lead.

Riding in a figure-of-eight is a very useful exercise for practising changing the diagonal at a trot and the lead leg at a canter. Trot a circle to the right, immediately followed by one to the left. As you change the rein at the point where the two circles in effect touch, change the diagonal. Follow this by cantering a right-handed circle, come back to a trot for a few paces at the centre of the figure-of-eight and 'strike off' on the left leg to canter a left-handed circle for the finish.

Trotting up and downhill helps to balance the pony's movement and the rider's position in the saddle.

The inside leg should always be the lead leg when cantering in a circle. If the pony leads with the outside leg, it will unbalance him.

Also practise changing the diagonal and lead leg while riding in a straight line down the school. Trot on one diagonal for a dozen or so strides, then change to the other. Canter for about the same distance, come back to a trot for a few strides and push into a canter with the other leg leading.

The aim is always to keep transitions from one pace to another as smooth and clearly defined as possible. For example, never break into a canter just by urging your pony ever faster at a trot, so that finally he has to canter. Providing he is moving forward in a balanced and disciplined trot, you should not have to increase the pace at all. Similarly, when slowing back down to a trot, do so as smoothly as possible, without giving a sharp pull on the reins, which will have the effect of jerking the pony's head.

The rein back

Another movement with which you should become familiar at this stage is the rein back, for there are many occasions when you may want your mount to go backwards for a few steps. The important thing about the rein back is that it is a pace in two-time. The pony moves opposite diagonal pairs of legs backwards together. However, unless he is properly collected and balanced and given the correct aids, he will 'walk' backwards in four-time, in an uneven, untidy movement.

Ask for a rein back from a halt, but make sure the pony is attentive. Close your legs against his sides and apply pressure with your seat as if pushing him forward into a walk. As you feel him responding to his aid and preparing to take a step forward, resist with your hands and lean very slightly forward. Having created the energy to move, but meeting the barrier of your hands, he will naturally step backwards. As soon as he has taken four or five steps backwards, push him forwards immediately. This is very important, for a pony should not get into the habit of moving backwards at will. If the final movement is forwards, the pony will remember this, above all.

Do's and don'ts

Do sit up straight in the deepest part of the saddle.

Do sit so there is a straight line from your shoulder through your elbow to your hips and down to your heel.

Do position the ball of your foot in the stirrup iron and keep your heel lower than your toe. Your foot should be parallel to the pony's side.

Don't grip the sides of the saddle with your knees and thighs. Keep them flat against the saddle but maintain your position through balance.

Don't grip the sides of the saddle with the back of your calves; your toes will turn out and your heels will dig into the pony's sides.

Don't slouch by rounding your shoulders and looking down at the ground.

The rein back is a pace in two-time, not four-time. When the pony has taken a few steps backwards make him walk forwards again.

Learning to jump

During the course of learning to ride, most good instructors will include some tuition on how to jump, providing the rider is keen to learn. Certainly by no means everybody who rides nurtures aspirations to be a great show-jumper – far from it. Indeed, some people never experience great enjoyment from jumping at all. On the other hand, many people get a tremendous thrill from jumping on horseback and find it the most exhilarating aspect of riding. In any event, it is useful to be able to sit a horse or pony with some measure of confidence as he pops over a small obstacle, for this may sometimes be necessary when out on a ride.

At its highest levels of competition, jumping is an extremely specialized and exacting sport, demanding great skill and talent from both horse and rider. However, almost all horses and ponies can negotiate small jumps and all riders can be taught how to go along with them. This is another case where the basics of learning to jump are the same for would-be international show jumpers as they are for those who want to do no more than be able to hop over the trunk of a fallen tree that obstructs their path during a ride.

It is wise not to attempt to jump until you really feel confident in the saddle of all paces and of all transitions. It is even more important now to have a secure seat and sympathetic, independent hands and for you to feel you can control your mount under most circumstances. If you do not feel so confident, do not be pushed into jumping. But do not feel you have to give up

the idea for all time either. Just work at the basic aspects of riding for a little longer.

The first thing you must get used to is the slightly altered position in the saddle that is universally adopted for jumping. This is known as the forward seat. As ever, it has been developed to give the pony the maximum assistance and freedom as he takes a jump. The stirrup leathers need to be shortened a couple of holes, but should still hang at right angles to the ground when your feet are in the irons. Your knees will,

therefore, be bent at a slightly more acute angle than for normal riding. Most of your weight is taken on your knees and heels in the jumping position, so keep your heels pressed well down. Your calves, knees and thighs should keep close contact with the saddle but, again, try to maintain your position through balance rather than grip. If you do have to grip, do so with your knees, not your calves.

It is the position of your upper body that alters most in the jumping position. Your back remains straight and

supple but your body is inclined forward from the hips so that your weight is supported on your thighs, knees, and heels, not your seat bones. Your head is held high as usual and you are again looking straight ahead between the pony's ears. This is of paramount importance. If you get into the habit of looking down at the fence or the ground, you will automatically round your shoulders and drop your body forward on one side.

Your arms are again bent at the elbow – avoid the common tendency to

LEFT: Most riders enjoy jumping but not everybody wants to enter competitions like this young rider. ABOVE: Buckle a neck strap round the pony's neck to hold on to while jumping. It helps to prevent you jerking him in the mouth.

let them stick out away from your sides – and there should still be a straight line running from the bit, through the reins and hands, to your elbows. It is extremely important in jumping to allow the pony complete freedom of his head. You should therefore move your hands forward on either side of his neck so that you do not interfere with his mouth. You will feel more secure and avoid jerking your pony in the mouth if you buckle a neckstrap about halfway along his neck. Hold on to the neckstrap, keeping a rein in each hand, through-

out the approach, take-off, suspension and landing over a jump. Alternatively, get hold of a good lock of mane halfway along the neck and do not let go!

Practise sitting in the forward position at a walk, trot and canter before attempting any obstacle, so that you get the feel of it thoroughly. When you become more confident you can begin to learn to jump. First, lay some thick, solid poles on the ground a good distance from one another and make your pony walk over them. A few strides in front of each one, assume the jumping position in the saddle and then return to the normal position a few strides after the pony has stepped over the pole. When you have got the feel of this (and it will not take long) repeat the exercise at a trot. You can then position the poles (use about six) equidistant from one another so that your horse trots over them one at a time with each step he takes.

Remember, you should feel secure and well-balanced in this new position at all times. If you suddenly realise that you are maintaining the position by tensing your muscles and gripping, go back to practising the position at the

various paces of walk, trot and canter. A good jumping position must rely on balance. Too much grip will quickly make your legs and body stiff and you will find it more difficult to follow the pony's movement sympathetically.

You can progress, from poles on the ground, to doing similar exercises over *cavalletti*. These are long poles attached at either end to a low support, which usually comprises two short planks joined together at the centre to form a cross. The poles are nailed to the cross in such a way that they can be placed on the ground at three different heights (see diagram, page 46): generally about 25 cm (10 in), 37.5 cm (15 in) and 47.5 cm (19 in). Cavalletti are most useful

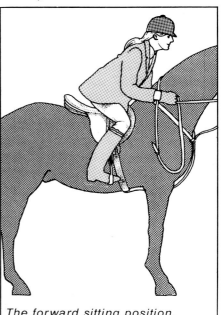

The forward sitting position.

items of equipment both for learning to jump and for training horses to jump. In fact, top-class show-jumpers generally include cavalletti work in the routine training of their horses.

Place four to six cavalletti in a straight line about 60–90 cm (2–3 ft) apart, so that the pony steps over one with each stride he takes. The distance will vary according to the length of your pony's stride and you may have to experiment a little to find the right distance. To begin with, put them at their lowest height and ask your pony to walk over them, adopting the forward position in exactly the same way as you did over the poles. At a walk, the pony will just step over each one, making no attempt to jump.

Make sure you ride in a straight line towards the middle of the cavalletti, so that the pony steps over the centre point of each one, maintaining sufficient impulsion to keep the pace even and steady throughout. Hold your

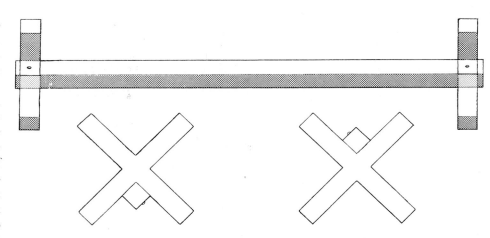

The diagram of a cavalletto illustrates the three possible positions.

Sit in the jumping position to trot over poles on the ground.

hands low on the neck so that the pony has complete freedom of his head – even at a walk he will stretch his neck and lower his head – and incline the upper part of your body to go with the movement of the pony. If you do not ride in a straight line towards the cavalletti and approach them at an angle, you will find the distances are incorrect for the pony's length of stride. The distance between the poles taken

on a slant will, of course, be greater.

As usual, once confident of this exercise, increase the distance between the cavalletti to accommodate a trotting stride. The cavalletti should now be about 1.2–1.5 m (4–4 ft 10 in) apart, depending upon the length of your pony's stride. It may be best to start off with three cavalletti only, positioned in a straight line, and work up to six by adding one more at a time.

Trotting over cavalletti is one of the most valuable exercises in learning how to jump.

Trotting over cavalletti in this way should really help you to develop and consolidate the forward jumping position. Approach the poles at a rising trot, keeping the pace controlled and even. Move into the forward position a stride or two before the cavalletti. Providing you keep the pony going forward at a regular pace, he will not need to jump the cavalletti but just to incorporate them in his stride. If he does hop over one, maintain your forward seat but drop your hands down his neck to ensure you do not let the jerky movement cause you to give him a jab in the mouth. Hang on to that lock of mane too, if you feel at all insecure.

There is an extremely good exercise you can try when you are confident about trotting over cavalletti. Knot your reins around the pony's neck, keeping hold of them as you approach the line, then drop them as your pony begins to move forward over the raised poles. Lean forward and fold your arms. Now you can feel whether your seat is secure and independent of your hands, for there is no way you can use your hands to help you keep your

balance, even on the sly. You will also find you need to keep up the energy and impulsion with your legs, since the loss of contact on the animal's mouth might encourage him to slacken his pace.

Next, you could try to canter over the cavelletti, moving them further apart as the cantering stride is longer. Alternatively, you could erect a low jump at the end of the line of cavalletti and trot your pony, first over the cavalletti and then on over the jump. In both instances, he will now jump rather than take the obstacles in his stride. For this reason, it may be useful to examine the action of a horse or pony as he makes a jump. Knowledge of his movement should help you to understand when you adopt the forward seat and how it helps the pony.

The five stages

The pony's action over a jump may be divided into five stages: the approach, take-off, suspension, landing and departure. The approach is the last few strides before the jump. It is the time when the pony balances himself ready for the ensuing spring off the ground. He will extend his neck and slightly lower his head, in order to help him assess the correct take-off point. He then pushes off from his hindquarters so

that his head and forehead lift to project him into the air. Finally, he springs off his hindlegs and they too leave the ground with sufficient propulsive force to carry him over the jump. During the suspension, the pony is on a horizontal plane but his neck is extended and his back slightly rounded so that his body forms an arc over the jump. (In this position, the pony is said to be 'basculating'.) All four legs are tucked well beneath him. As he begins his descent, he again stretches his neck forward and downward. His shoulders descend and his forelegs stretch out down towards the ground (generally one foreleg lands fractionally before the other), his head comes up and his neck shortens, or retracts, a little. Often, he will begin the departure from the jump with one foreleg before his hindlegs have touched the ground. His first strides away from the jump should, in any event, be in exact line with his approach.

Relate your position in the saddle throughout the jump to the movement described above. As the pony approaches the jump, you assume the forward position so that, in effect, you are a little ahead of him. In this way, he has complete freedom for the take-off. During suspension, there is nothing you can do to assist the pony actively. In fact, any movement you make could severely throw him off balance. You should therefore remain quite still in the forward position, your hands pushed well forward up his neck. Your position during landing is equally critical. You may feel you want to lean back to balance the downward movement. But this is totally wrong. If you do sit back in the saddle too soon, your weight may make the pony drop his hindquarters prematurely, quite possibly on to the jump. The other temptation is to use the reins to steady yourself, but this, too, should of course be avoided. The action of the hind legs touching the ground and the pony moving forward will automatically push you back into the saddle into the normal riding position.

The forward position

It is important in jumping, perhaps more than in any other branch of riding, not to interfere with the pony or cause him any pain or discomfort. If jumping begins to have unhappy associations for him, he will soon become reluctant to jump at all. This would be a great pity for, if treated sympathetically, most horses and ponies enjoy jumping as much as their riders.

When you have studied the pony's movement and your position in relation to it, try the exercise of trotting over two or three cavalletti with a small jump positioned after them. The jump should be no more than 60 cm (2 ft). Trot over the cavalletti, sitting in the jumping position and maintaining impulsion all the time, and stay in the forward position as the pony pops over the jump at the end. Seeing a jump at the end of the row of cavalletti may encourage the pony to increase his speed, even breaking into a canter, as he approaches the poles. Try to restrain him before you reach the cavalletti, but on no account haul on the reins in the middle of the line. If he does increase his pace at this point just drop your hands down, in order not to interfere with his head, and maintain the forward position so that you go with the movement over the jump. Once confident of this exercise

Note how the rider is giving the pony complete freedom of his head as he jumps this gate.

Taking a jump can be broken down into five parts – approach, take-off, suspension, landing and departure. The rider should be in the forward position so as not to interfere with the pony's movement.

with cavalletti, you can begin to build some small practice jumps around the field.

In spite of the seemingly enormous variety of jumps seen in the show-ring or on event courses, there are, in fact, only two basic types of fence: uprights and spreads. From these have developed the endless permutations which, in their simpler form, you should copy to make practice jumps.

Practice jumps

Upright fences include single poles or a series of poles suspended one on top of another from the same side-supports, walls, gates, narrow brush fences and other similar vertical constructions. Spread fences are much more varied. Parallel bars, triple bars, placed in ascending order of height or with the middle bar in the highest position, and 'oxers', consisting of a hedge flanked on one or both sides by a pole either at the same height or lower than the hedge, are just some of them.

Place your jumps around the field or space available to you, using your imagination and whatever materials you can lay your hands on to make them as varied as possible. Old doors or stepladders – provided they have no splintery edges or rusty, protruding nails – bundles of twigs or small branches, old car tyres, oil-drums, cans and wooden boxes can all be made into jumps. Moreover, a couple of pots of paint can make the whole effort look quite professional.

Try to make the jumps look fairly solid rather than flimsy. Horses and ponies are cunning creatures. They will have little regard for a frail-looking fence, knowing that if they hit it, or even push their way through it, it will give way easily enough. They will always jump a solid-looking fence better and more boldly, which will help you to gain more confidence.

Keep the fences 60–90 cm (2–3 ft) high for the time being. If you can make them adjustable and if they collapse

when given a hefty kick, so much the better. If not, keep them to the lower height.

It helps a horse or pony to judge his take-off point if a pole or similar marker is placed in front of him, particularly if the fence is an upright one. With some variation, depending on the size of the fence and the speed of the animals, the take-off point should be approximately the same distance away from the fence as the height of the fence from the ground. Thus a 90 cm (3 ft) high fence should have a groundline pole placed 90 cm (3 ft) in front of it.

Another way to encourage a pony to steady himself before a jump is to put a single cavalletto a couple of strides in front. You will probably need to experi-

ment to get the right distance for the stride, as a single canter stride may vary from about 2.4–4.2 m (8–14 ft). You have also to take into account how far away from the cavalletto he will land and the point of take-off for the jump. Normally, 5–6 m (17–20 ft) will be about the right distance. This small arrangement of a cavalletto placed in front of a larger jump will begin to give you the feel of jumping 'combinations', a term used to describe two or three fences placed in line with one or two strides between the fences.

Build some jumps in the area of the field for practice. Use your imagination to vary them.

One of your constant aims in jumping should be to approach your fences in the centre. A jump that will greatly assist you in judging this in your early attempts is a simple one made with two crossed poles. Support each pole at the same height at one end only, letting the other end rest on the ground. If the poles are of even length, the point at which they cross will be the middle. This will, of course, also be part of the fence and the most attractive point for the pony to jump.

If possible, include a ditch and a bank in your range of jumps. (You could make the bank with the earth dug out of the ditch!) Horses and ponies are often very suspicious of jumping holes

in the ground and will snort nervously on the edge before making a horrendous cat leap with all four feet leaving the ground. If the ditch is not very wide, it is better to keep urging your mount forward when he stops on the edge rather than turning him round to try again. Just hang on to his mane for all you are worth so that, when he finally makes his leap upward and forward, you do not jab him in the mouth. A water-filled ditch is, by the way, better than a dry one. Horses and ponies should get accustomed to jumping water, so as to prepare them for those occasions when it may be essential to do so.

The way a horse or pony jumps a

bank will depend to some extent on the size of the bank. If it is small enough to jump like a normal fence, this is probably the way he will take it. It is more usual, however, to jump up on to the top of the bank and then jump down off the other side in one continuous movement. Be prepared for this the first time you put your pony at a bank. It can be a little unseating if you are not expecting it! So be warned!

Important points

Think of the important points you have learned about jumping as you start to practise your jumps. These are summarized below:

Assume the jumping position in the

53

saddle a few strides before the jump and return to your normal position in the saddle a few strides after landing.

Keep looking straight ahead between the pony's ears – never down at the fence.

Try to maintain your position through balance rather than by grip but, if grip is essential, do so with your knees not with the lower part of your legs.

Keep your heels pressed down and your ankles supple and relaxed as they will take the jar of landing.

Push your hands forward to eliminate any possible danger of jabbing the pony in the mouth and try to approach all your fences in the centre.

Bear in mind, too, that the actual time of suspension is very short, but it is essential that you sit absolutely still. Never try to use that moment to regain your balance or you could seriously upset the pony's landing.

Initially, your jumping practice will probably be confined to two or three jumps – crossed poles, a line of straw bales, some low parallel bars, perhaps – all of which you will jump as single fences with the constant aim of improving your position and performance.

Never overdo your practice so that your pony, and probably you too, become bored and mechanical in what you are doing. And do not be tempted to keep raising the height of the fences if you appear to be making light of them. It is much better to widen the spread so that your horse has to extend himself further over the jump, which in turn will give you as the rider a greater feel of the jumping action.

Building a course

When you sense that you are gaining confidence, try building a small course of jumps. Include a variety of uprights and spreads and arrange them in such a way that you can jump them in a number of different sequences. In this way, again, your pony is less likely to get bored. If, on the other hand, he gets to know the way to go round the jumps because you never change it, he will just jump them as a matter of routine, taking you round with no conscious effort on your part at all. Obviously this will do neither of you any good.

Illustrated (opposite page) is a course

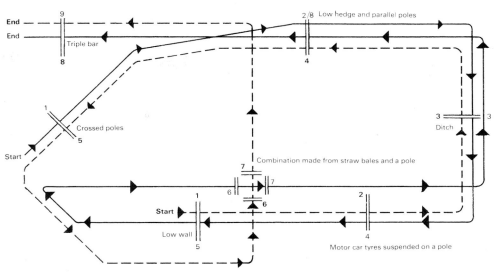

Diagram of a jumping course.

of eight jumps (counting the combination jump as two) which you could construct in an area of about 50 m × 30 m (152 ft × 100 ft), using fairly makeshift materials. Remember to keep them all under 90 cm (3 ft) initially. Two possible routes are outlined, but obviously there are many more you could take as well. The course is quite versatile, in that the only jump that has to be taken in just one direction is the triple bar. All the others can be jumped from either side.

Try the course given as an unbroken line first. This way you begin with a jump of crossed poles which makes an easy beginning for you and your pony. Fence 2 is a low hedge flanked on either side with parallel poles of the same height. You can increase the width of these as you get more confident. Next, swing in a wide circle to the right so that you approach obstacle 3, a narrow ditch, with a good straight run up to it. From there swing in another right-handed arc to approach fence 4, car tyres suspended from a pole. You could balance the pole on oil-drums, or from jump supports, but keep it low so that the tyres are only just clear of the ground. Fence 5 is a low wall or, if you prefer, you could put a gate or similar upright here. If you do construct a wall, use wooden planks or a sheet of plywood or hardboard painted to look like a wall. Do not use bricks or stones; they are too hard and sharp if your

A combination fence consists of two or three jumps so as to give one or two strides between each.

pony should hit them. After this fence, turn right again so that you approach the combination in the middle of the course from as far away as possible, with a straight line of approach. The first part of the combination could be just a single line of straw bales placed on the ground, while the second part, which should be sufficiently far away to allow a single stride in between landing and take-off, could be a line of straw bales with a pole suspended over them. The second part of a combination fence is usually higher than the first but, in this instance, it is not advisable to increase the height by adding another row of bales on top. If a pony does knock a bale with his hindlegs it could easily get tangled up in his legs and make him fall. After the combination, change the rein by going round the ditch left-handed and take fence 2 again the other way. This gives you a good straight line of approach to the final fence – the triple bar.

For the broken-line course shown swing the straw bales of the combination round so they are at right angles to their original position, then follow the course as it is marked. This time, you start with the wall, so, bearing in mind that the first jump of a course should never be too demanding or difficult, it is wise to construct a low one. The jumps are taken in reverse order from Course 1 except for the triple bar, which must be jumped this way. If the crossed poles seem a little easy now, turn them into a vertical with

If a pony runs out at a fence, try constructing large wings on either side to discourage him.

one pole on top of the other or into a low, but fairly wide, parallel. The ditch, too, you can make a little more interesting by suspending a pole over the top of it, in the centre.

Try taking other lines around the course – you will find there are numerous alternatives. You can equally well change the position of the jumps from time to time. With the exception of the

ditch, they can all be moved easily. This not only helps to vary the jumping sessions for you and your pony, it also pevents the ground from becoming too churned up or muddy on either side of the fences.

Remember, when planning your day's riding activity, that if you wish to include a jumping session around your course, it should always follow a short spell of schooling or limbering up your pony at a walk, trot and canter. Never take a horse or pony fresh from the stable or field to a jumping paddock

and expect him to start leaping over fences without first giving him a chance to loosen up a little.

Although it is fun and enjoyable to jump, the aim of your practice sessions should be to improve you and your pony's combined performance. Try to think about what you are doing and the areas you need to work at to improve. Do not, at these times, attempt to jump ever bigger fences that may be beyond you or your pony's capabilities. You are much more likely to be able to jump them competently before long if you do the basic groundwork now.

If your pony seems very keen and excitable at the beginning of a jumping session, work him a bit longer at a good, balanced trot and canter or go back to trotting over a row of cavalletti which often has a calming effect.

Practise jumping from a trot as well as a canter. As none of the jumps in your course should be very big, your pony should be able to take them all quite easily from a trot. Go round the

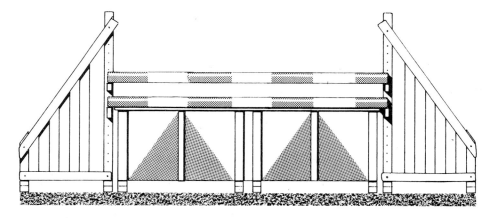

A jump with wings at either side.

jumps at the slower pace first and, provided you are in full control, repeat the course at a canter.

It is possible that sooner or later your pony will refuse at a jump. There are many reasons why this may happen. It may be that the pony is bored with jumping the same jump over and over again or that you have raised the jump too rapidly. He may have approached it out of balance so that his instinct tells him it is better to stop than to attempt an unsuccessful jump; or, if you are feeling nervous, you may well transmit this to your mount and make him loose his confidence.

Some recommend that if the jump is small, you should back the pony a few steps after a refusal and then urge him forward forcefully. Although he probably will jump the fence, this is not a very satisfactory way of tackling the problem as it can easily instil the idea of backing away from an obstacle into the animal's mind. Instead, therefore, turn him away and ride in a small circle, so that you re-present him at the fence quickly and in a straight line of approach. Make the approach short, rather than riding him towards the fence from the other side of the field and giving him lots of time to look for other distractions or plan some way of escape!

You will generally be able to tell if your pony is planning to refuse. He has to lower his head to stop. If you feel him beginning to slow down and his head dropping downwards, urge him forward more strongly with your seat and legs.

The other common way for a pony to avoid jumping is to run out to one side at the very last moment of approach. Constructing wings on both sides of a fence can help to stop this. Cavalletti are very useful. Prop one end up against the sides of the jump and let the other end slope to the ground at an angle coming forward from the jump.

If your pony should start to acquire this habit, turn him round in the opposite direction and then approach the jump again at a slight angle from the side where he ran out. If, for example, he tends to run out to the left, turn him to the right, ride a small circle and drive him at the jump coming in from the left.

Whatever problems either you or your pony may have encountered at

your jumping session, always finish with a good jump. Reward your pony by patting him and making a fuss of him. Slacken off his girth and perhaps let him have a mouthful or two of grass before returning to the stable yard or turning him out in his field.

You do not have to be very experienced to enter some of the competitions at a local gymkhana. In jumping events, give your number to the organizer, who will write up the order of jumping on a board in the collecting ring.

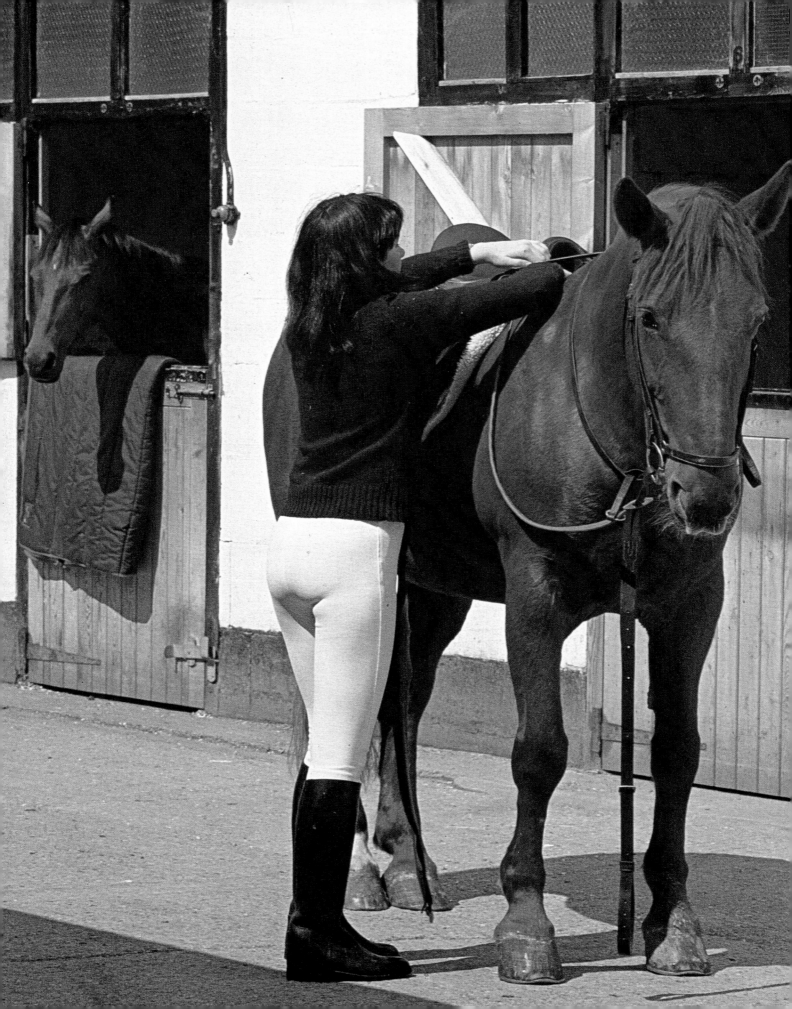

3 The stable-kept pony

Keeping horses or ponies stabled really means depriving them of their natural outdoor environment, for the ponies and few horses that are still to be found living 'wild' survive winter and summer with only the shelter they can find from trees, rocks or bushes. Many of today's carefully bred thoroughbred horses or show-type ponies are too sensitive and thin-skinned to survive the rigours of harsh winter conditions and need to lead a more pampered indoor life.

Keeping horses indoors originates from the days when transport depended on horsepower. It was essential to have horses available to pull a cab or carriage and the only way to ensure this was for them to be ready to hand in a stable, not wet and muddy in some far-off field. In those days, however, there were plenty of people to look after the horses. It was a very different story from the owner-groom situation that generally applies today.

Horses need a great deal of care and attention, so do consider the amount of time you can spare if you are thinking of keeping either a horse or a pony stabled. Stabled animals are generally fitter, more accessible, cleaner and more respectable in appearance than their grass-kept relatives but there is a price to pay for such advantages. Besides being more costly to keep, stabled animals must be fed three or four times a day at regular intervals, exercised for at leat an hour (and preferably longer) each day, given daily, thorough grooming and kept in clean, hygienic conditions. This means the regular mucking-out of their stables. Unless you keep them on a 'combined system' (see page 88), there are no short cuts to this work and it is very time-consuming.

The first requirement for keeping a horse or pony stabled is some sort of stable building. Conventional stabling varies considerably in design and construction, but there are two main types

The advantage of a stable-kept pony is that he is ready to hand whenever you want him.

Being able to look out onto a busy yard helps to alleviate boredom for a stabled pony.

of stable – stalls and loose boxes. Stalls are now regarded as rather old-fashioned. Generally, several stalls are contained within a building and each one consists of a three-sided compartment in which the horse has to be kept tied up, his head to the wall. Behind him is a passage which gives access to all the stalls. A loose box is, in effect, a self-contained room in which a horse has greater freedom since he does not have to be tied. This means he can move around and even lie down if he chooses, which obviously makes it preferable to the stall arrangement.

Loose boxes can either be free-standing buildings or several can be housed within one large building. In the latter event, each has its own door so that the horse or pony looks out on to a passage way. Loose boxes that open directly on to an outside yard are best. Most stabled horses and ponies are

happier if they can look out and see what is happening in the yard. This helps to prevent boredom, which is one of the greatest problems that has to be overcome in keeping animals stabled.

Minimum size

A loose box must be big enough to allow the horse or pony to turn around comfortably without knocking himself against the wall and he must also be able to lie down easily. There should be sufficient room, too, for him to get back to his feet. This may seem obvious, but a horse can lie down in a space which proves to be too small to allow him to get up again. A loose box for a horse should be at least 4.2 m × 3.6 m (14 ft × 12 ft). A pony needs slightly less room – 3.6 m × 3 m (12 ft × 10 ft) would be sufficient. In both instances the box must be high enough to allow the animal to lift up his head without hitting it on the ceiling.

If the stable opens straight on to the outside world it should ideally face south, which offers the most shelter from severe weather conditions. If, for example, the stable were to face north, it would be directly exposed to cold winds. The door is generally constructed in two parts and the top half is kept permanently open, hooked back against the wall. This allows in light and a good supply of fresh air as well as giving the stabled animal a chance to look out. Both parts of the door should open outwards and swing right back to the stable's outer wall. Opening outwards is important since it allows you to open the door without disturbing the bedding, but also gives access to the stable when the pony is lying down against the door. This may be necessary if he is 'cast', that is, unable to get up, for any reason. The doorway should be wide enough for both you and the pony to pass through side-by-side without one or other of you banging yourself on the frame. It should therefore be at least 1.2 m (4 ft) wide. All bolts, latches and catches should be on the outside of the door to protect the pony from injury if he scrapes against them and to eliminate any possibility of his learning how to open them, which is far from unknown. The bottom door has two bolts, one at the top and one at the bottom, and they should both be secured when the pony is inside. Special 'kick' catches are useful for the bottom door. These swing, rather than slide, into place and can be operated by the foot. Stable bolts must be strong. They have to withstand repeated use and often considerable pressure if the horse or pony likes to lean against the door.

Ventilation and light

Ventilation of the stable is very important as a means of providing both a constant supply of fresh air and also adequate lighting. Fresh air is vital to a horse's health. If the atmosphere is stuffy and unpleasant, coughs and colds soon develop.

Leaving the top half of the door open is obviously a help in providing both ventilation and light, but there should also be a window. Ideally, this should be located in the wall alongside the door and situated above the animal's head. The best type of windows are those that are hinged 30 cm (1 ft) or so from the top and open inwards. This provides ventilation without draughts

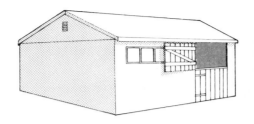

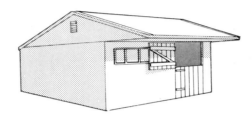

Two types of loose boxes.

The door of a stable is always constructed in two parts and the top should be hooked open permanently (big picture). The lower door has two bolts (page 61), the bottom one being a swing catch (far right). The window is barred to prevent any danger of a pony breaking the glass (below left). The three-cornered manger shown here has a removable feed bowl for ease of cleaning (second from left).

as the fresh air enters the stable in an upward direction. It is essential that there are no draughts. Draughty stables will soon lead to health problems. The glass should be protected by bars on the inside so that the pony cannot reach it. Remember to keep the window clean or it will not do its job of admitting light.

It is a good idea to have an electric light in the stable. The bulb should be high enough to prevent the horse from touching it, even if he stretches up his head. However, just in case he can reach it, it should be encased in a wire cage. This also reduces any risk of fire should any wisps of hay or straw fly up and touch the bulb when you are

Bales of wood shavings for bedding are bulky to store. Strong polythene protects the contents.

shaking the bedding or tying up the hay net.

The floor should not be slippery or affected by moisture. Ideally, the floor should be made of material that dries quickly and be very slightly sloped so that it drains easily. At one time, stable floors were always constructed of special stable bricks but these are now expensive and are also quite difficult to keep clean. Roughened concrete is satisfactory and meets the requirements of being waterproof, non-slip and fairly hard-wearing.

Stable fittings

Although some fittings within the stable are essential, they should otherwise be kept to a minimum. The more things there are around, the greater are the chances of horses or ponies injuring

themselves on them. The bare essentials are a ring for tethering the pony and another for securing the hay net. Feeding and watering can be carried out in removable containers. This makes the cleaning of the stable easier, but it is not always considered satisfactory since many horses and ponies will tip over free-standing boxes or buckets and spill their feed into the bedding. Many stables are equipped with some sort of fixed manger, usually positioned at the animal's chest level. This is often placed in a corner and the food may be either tipped in or provided in a bowl which fits into the manger bracket. The latter is more satisfactory from the point of view of cleaning the feed bowl. Besides being positioned at a comfortable height for eating, a manger must not have any sharp edges which can cause cuts or bruises, nor should it be too narrow or so deep that the animal cannot reach into it without difficulty.

The other consideration is how to provide a constant supply of fresh water. Automatic watering systems are available, whereby a lever or disc is activated as the water level drops. However, they are not easy to clean and they must be frequently checked to make sure they are working properly. A better way of providing water is in a strong rubber bucket placed in a corner of the stable. A bracket fixed to the wall in which the bucket sits is a good idea since this ensures that the water is not tipped over at any time. All water containers should be scrubbed out thoroughly at least once a week.

Hay nets

Old stables and stalls were usually fitted with hay racks placed high up on the wall so that the horse or pony had to stretch up to pull at the hay. Today these are frowned upon since dust and hay seeds fall directly on to the pony's face as he pulls at the hay. The best way to feed hay is in a hay net. This should be tied securely to a ring positioned in the wall about level with the pony's head.

Since it would be most uncomfortable for a horse or pony to have to stand on a bare floor throughout the day and night, some sort of covering or bedding must be put down. Various materials

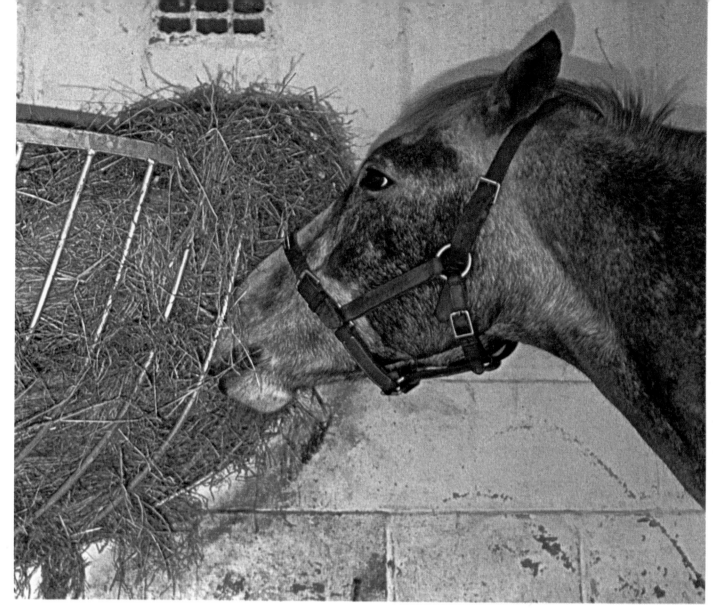

Some stables still have hay racks although it is more usual to feed hay in a net.

are used, most frequently straw, peat, wood shavings or sawdust. Straw is probably the most satisfactory of these and wheat straw is the best of all. Oat and barley straw are also available but horses and ponies find oat straw rather tasty, so using it encourages them to eat their bedding. Besides being wasteful, this often causes coughing. Barley straw has rather long hairs which can irritate the skin of a sensitive animal. If eaten it is liable to cause colic, too (see page 97), and it has a tendency to harbour lice. Wheat straw should be bright yellow in colour and should have a pleasant smell. If it is black in parts, mouldy or smells musty, it should not be used. Old straw, provided it has been stored in

clean, dry conditions, is preferable to newly harvested straw.

Peat makes a perfectly satisfactory bedding material, but in some areas it can be expensive to buy. Peat is very absorbent but it is often hard to see the wet or soiled patches since it is so dark in colour. If peat is used then, particular care must be taken in mucking out the stable. If the peat is allowed to remain wet and soggy it can affect the pony's feet.

Sawdust beds

Wood shavings or sawdust make good beds, particularly for those animals that tend to eat straw bedding. However, besides often causing blocked drains because of the way it 'clogs' when it is wet, sawdust is inclined to heat up very quickly as it gets damp. This again is bad for the horse or pony's

feet. Sawdust beds must be kept as clean as possible and the large amount of replenishment needed on each occasion can provide storage problems unless you have a timber yard close by.

Since the stabled horse is deprived of his normal grass diet, great care must be taken to feed him properly. Before looking at the types of foodstuff, however, we must explain a set of rules for feeding with which every would-be horseman or horsewoman should be familiar.

The first of these is to feed little and often. Horses are grazers by nature and constant nibbling means that there is nearly always some food present in their stomachs. In fact, a horse's stomach is remarkably small for the size of the animal. If he bolts down a large meal because he has been deprived of food for some time and is very hungry,

Galvanized iron feed bins are easy to keep clean and also vermin-proof.

not only will his stomach be stretched to its limits, but it may not be able to accommodate all the food he consumes. This will result in an attack of colic.

Always feed each day at the same time so that the horse knows when he may expect his meals. You can fix the times to suit yourself and your daily routine, but once you have established a timetable, you should stick to it.

Use only good quality food. Old or stale food will have a low nutritive value. Horses are fussy feeders and will probably not touch bad food. On the other hand, if hunger drives them to eat bad food then it is likely to prove harmful. Equally, do not make sudden changes in the diet. If you want to feed some other sort of foodstuff, make the changeover gradually so that the animal has a chance to become accustomed to his new diet over a period of days.

Feed your horse something succulent in the way of vegetables, apples or green food each day. Give him lots of bulk, or 'roughage', provided in the form of hay. A stabled horse should always have a plentiful supply of hay so that he can nibble at it as he feels inclined. Concentrated food should be mixed with roughage, either as chaff (chopped hay) or bran (see page 65).

A golden rule

Feed according to the amount of work expected from the animal and according to his condition. A horse that is being ridden hard, perhaps in competition, racing or hunting, will need more food than a horse required only for gentle hacking. Similarly, a horse or pony in bad condition will need a carefully planned programme of nutritious body-building foodstuffs.

Do not work a horse or pony immediately after a large feed. He needs a couple of hours or so in which to digest his food. It will cause him great discomfort to go for a hard ride on a full stomach. Do let him eat in peace. Once you have given his feed, leave him alone in the stable. Do not choose this time to groom him or to renew his bedding.

The final golden rule is to make sure your horse has had ample opportunity to drink before feeding, so that the food is not washed straight through his stomach. The first rule of watering – which cannot be stressed too often – is that a constant supply of clean, fresh water should always be available. If for any reason this is not possible, a stabled animal should be given a bucket of fresh water at least three times a day in winter and six times a day in the summer. If water is not provided continuously in the stable, allow a good half hour to elapse after a pony has finished his feed before letting him drink.

If a horse or pony is brought in very hot from work and the water is very icy, it may be warmed slightly. However, this is the only time water should be warmed artificially. Icy water in a drinking trough in a field does not harm a grass-kept animal in the least.

Water in the stable, which tends to absorb ammonia and other impurities present in the air, should be renewed at least three times a day. Finally, if you are going to ask your horse or pony to work hard, remove the water bucket so that he cannot drink for the previous two to three hours. During the course of a long day's work – say, at a show or when hunting – allow your horse only a short drink at any given time, not a long draught.

Of the concentrated grain food fed to horses and ponies as supplementary feeding, oats are the best energy-producer. Great care should be taken if feeding oats to ponies since they tend to make them very excitable. It is generally better, in fact, to give small ponies other types of grain.

Oats may be given whole or crushed. Crushed oats are easier for a horse to digest, but ideally they should be bought whole and crushed on the premises. After two or three weeks crushed oats begin to lose their nutritive value. Oats should always be plump, heavy, sweet-smelling and of a good, bright, colour. Avoid those that smell mouldy or those which have a large percentage of stalks, seeds or bits of grit or earth among them.

Nutritive foods

The other concentrated foods that may be fed are barley, flaked maize or beans, none of which measure up to oats as producers of energy. Boiled barley is a good food for a horse that is out of condition and needs fattening. Maize is also a fattening food and is not very suitable for horses doing a great deal of work or for those doing very little. Beans are rich in nutriment and should really only be fed to horses that are badly out of condition or ones that are being worked extremely hard. Beans can be very 'heating', and can make a horse both excitable and hard to control.

Probably the most commonly used nutritive foodstuffs in recent years are the commercially prepared horse and pony cubes. Several different varieties are available, the content depending upon whether they are to be fed, for example, to ponies, mares-in-foal or racehorses. In essence they are all compounds made up of various ingredients with added vitamins and minerals. They are the most convenient foodstuff to give as they dispense with the necessity of mixing feeds and ensure a constant and balanced diet. In addition, they will take up less storage space than the numbers of different foodstuffs needed to produce their equivalent. However, there are one or two factors to bear in mind about feeding cubes. First, they tend to have a low moisture content, which means it is even more vital to ensure that a good supply of water is always present. Some roughage such as bran should also be fed with them, or the animal may gobble them down too quickly and so give himself colic. Feeding cubes gives you less control over the exact constituents of the animal's diet since these are already predetermined and, lastly, they are probably the most expensive way of feeding.

As mentioned earlier, bran is the commonest roughage to mix with concentrated food and is probably used instead of chaff in most modern stables. Bran is the outer husk of wheat and is a by-product produced in the milling of flour. It can be fed as a mash, in which case it is mixed with hot water and allowed to cool. This is very digestible and has a laxative effect, making it suitable for a sick animal or an animal that is tired after a spell of very hard work.

The major bulk feed for horses and ponies is, of course, hay, of which there are two main types – seed hay and meadow hay. Seed hay is sown as a rotation crop and varies according to the seed. Those commonly sown are Sainfoin, or Timothy, clover or a special mixture. All provide good hay, although clover is perhaps the richest. Meadow hay is cut from land that is

An owner-groom takes a full hay net to a pony who is waiting patiently.

permanent pasture and it therefore varies considerably in content. It usually contains a higher percentage of grasses than seed hay, making it greener in colour.

Whatever kind of hay is fed, it should smell sweet, without a trace of mustiness. The hay will vary a little in colour according to its content. It may be golden, light brown or green. If it is yellow or dark brown, then it has deteriorated in quality. It should always look bright and clean. When you shake it, dust should not fly out in great clouds.

Various other foodstuffs may be given to horses and ponies. Linseed, for example, may be fed to improve condition, but remember that it must first be cooked, otherwise it is poisonous. Sugar beet pulp and molasses are nutritious and the sweet taste of molasses, in particular, can be used to make other foodstuffs more attractive to a fussy eater. Sugar beet must be soaked overnight to allow it to swell to its full extent. Root vegetables, such as carrots, mangolds, swedes and turnips,

A pony who has been clipped out must be kept warm with rugs and extra blankets.

parsnips and beetroot, are all good succulent foods. They should always be sliced lengthwise or fed whole. When they are cut into rounds or cubes they can get stuck in the animal's throat.

It is almost impossible to advise on how much feed should be provided, for so much depends on individual cases. Besides the size of the horse or pony and how hard he is working, there is his general physical condition to consider and whether, quite simply, he has a big appetite. Horses and ponies vary as much as people in the amount of food they need to keep them going through the day.

Quantities also depend on the type of food. A 14.2 h.h. (hands high, see page 143) pony kept stabled in the winter and doing reasonably hard, regular work, would need about 3–3.6 kg (6½–9 lb) of concentrated food a day, mixed with about 1.4 kg (3 lb) bran. This would be a large quantity of oats to give a pony, so it might be better to feed half oats and half cubes, or all cubes. The food should be given in three or four feeds. The largest feed should be in the evening, thus giving a long restful time for digestion as well as a substantial feed to last through the night. In addition to the concentrated

food, the pony would need about 6.5 kg (15 lb) of hay, probably in three haynets through the day.

Rugs and 'clothing'

Before looking in some detail at the daily routine of stabled horses and ponies, we might consider the clothing that should be provided for them. In summer, rugs for additional warmth are generally unnecessary. A light cotton rug, or 'summer sheet', may be worn if you want to keep dust off a freshly-groomed coat, but its main purpose is to keep an animal clean and unbothered by flies at a show or during transportation. A summer sheet follows the conventional pattern of a rug. It covers the back to the tail and the sides of the body to the top of the legs and is held in place by a buckle at the chest and by a light girth or surcingle that buckles round the tummy. It also has a 'fillet string' which is joined to the sides of the rug at the back and lies just above the hocks under the tail. Its purpose is to prevent the rug blowing up in a summer breeze.

In winter, a stabled pony must be protected against cold weather. The number of rugs, or more accurately blankets, worn under the rug, will

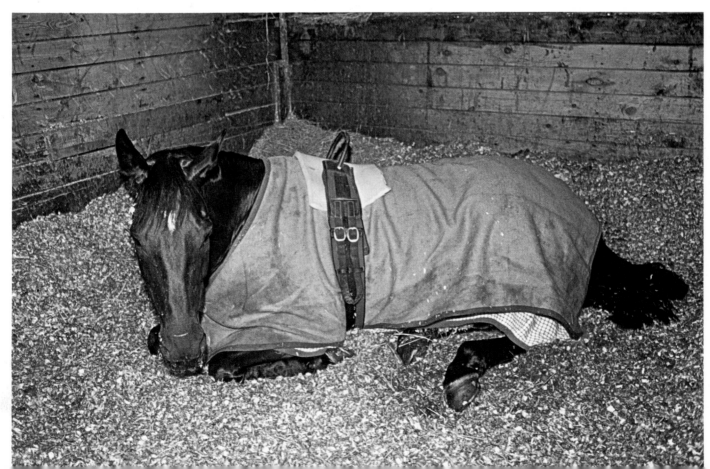

depend on whether the animal has been clipped or not. Clipping is the process of removing the coat, which gives the animal a smarter appearance but leaves him exposed to harsh weather conditions. A horse or pony's coat may be clipped off entirely, or the legs and a patch of hair the shape of the saddle may be left unclipped. Sometimes a 'blanket' of hair is left on the back and sides, affording the animal some natural protection. Alternatively, the hair may be clipped from the belly, flanks, lower part of the shoulders and underneath the neck only. This is known as a 'trace clip' and is suitable for ponies that are going to spend most of their time out in the field. It makes them look a little smarter than if the coat is left on entirely and prevents them from sweating and heating up too much if ridden hard during the winter.

Day and night rugs

Two basic rugs are needed for the stabled animal. These are the day rug and the night rug. Day rugs are made of woollen material and are bound round the edges, usually with braid of a contrasting colour. A matching roller keeps the rug in position, encircling the back at its deepest point behind the withers and buckling at the side. Rollers usually have extra padding either side of the spine to protect the spine. Day rugs are something of a luxury item, normally worn only if the animal is to be 'on show' for any reason.

The night rug is made of coarse hemp or jute lined with woollen material and is generally worn day and night by most stabled animals. Each animal should have at least two rugs in this instance, so that they can be changed morning and evening. A night rug will withstand a certain amount of moisture and damp if the animal lies down, but it will need fairly frequent washing to keep it clean and hygienic. Blankets may be put under the night rug to give additional warmth. Proper horse blankets are made of pure wool and are usually fawn coloured, with striped edges. They are expensive and, in fact, any woollen blanket will suffice.

To put on a rug, fold the back half forward over the front half. Then, standing on the nearside, throw the rug over the pony's withers so that the front

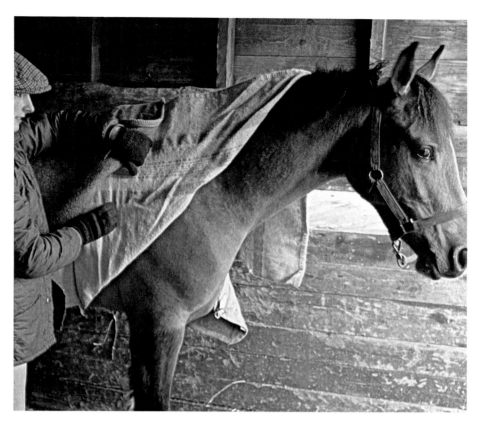

TOP: This horse has been clipped out and is wearing a rug for extra protection. ABOVE and RIGHT: Stable bandages both protect the legs and keep them warm.

is well forward on the neck. Fold the back half down over the loins and hindquarters and then pull the rug into place from behind the animal. The front of the rug should just cover the withers. Pulling it backwards like this ensures that the hair is lying flat. Make sure the central seam runs straight along the horse's spine before doing up the chest buckle and then putting the roller in place and buckling that, too.

The roller does not need to be as tightly fastened as the girths on a saddle.

If a blanket is to be worn beneath the rug, it should be thrown over the back in the same way, but make sure it is well up the neck. Also ensure that there is an even amount on either side. Put the rug on top as usual and, after buckling the chest strap, fold the blanket back over the front of the rug like a collar. Finally, buckle the roller into position.

To take off a rug, remove the roller and undo the front buckle. Fold the front half back and then pull the rug off towards the back, so as not to ruffle the hair up the wrong way.

Occasional bandages are worn by stabled animals on the lower part of

Wood shaving will pack tightly into the bottom of a pony's hoof and must be removed daily.

their legs for warmth and protection. Stable bandages are made of woollen material and have tapes sewn to one end. They must be put on carefully. Bandages should be sufficiently tight to ensure they stay in place but not so tight that they in any way interfere with the circulation in the leg. Cotton wool may be placed round the leg underneath the bandages to give extra warmth or protection.

The correct way to put on stable bandages is shown in the photographs, but before you put them on make sure they are correctly rolled. They should be rolled from the end with the tapes, these being folded neatly with the sewn side inside. When wound round the leg, the end of the bandage will then lie flat against the side of the leg. The tapes should always be tied in a knot on the outside of the pony's leg and the ends tucked in. If they are tied on the inside, they could come undone if one leg rubs constantly against the other. If they are tied on the front or back of the leg, they could press against a tendon and cause discomfort or pain.

The daily routine follows a similar pattern for all stabled animals and generally begins early. The procedure outlined below presumes you have the major part of the day free to look after your pony. Obviously the routine may have to be modified to fit in with school or other commitments.

You should first visit the stable at about 7.00 a.m. Examine the pony to make sure he has not hurt himself in the night, perhaps by knocking or scraping himself against the stable wall. Adjust his rugs to make him comfortable, then give him some fresh water and a small net of hay. Pick out his feet (tie him up first if necessary) and proceed to muck out the stable.

Mucking out

Mucking out entails removing the soiled bedding and is probably among the least pleasant, if most necessary, of stable chores. Remove any large patches of soiled straw or any dung, using a fork, and put it all straight into a wheelbarrow (or a sheet of sacking kept for this purpose) placed at the stable door. Shake out the clean bedding, using either a four-pronged fork or a pitchfork, and stack it up loosely at the back of the stable. Sweep the floor and leave it free of straw for a while to give it a chance to dry off and air. The dirty straw should be taken to the manure heap and stacked neatly so that the heap always has a flat top and vertical sides. This helps to keep it looking neat and also assists in the decomposing process. Horse manure makes excellent garden fertilizer and you will find keen gardeners are always eager to buy it. You will also find that this can be quite a helpful source of income.

First grooming

After mucking out, the pony should receive his first grooming of the day. This, however, is a very superficial operation, done to make him look respectable for the morning exercise and to remove any stains he may have incurred by lying down in the night. It is known as 'quartering' and is carried out without removing or even undoing the rugs. Sponge the eyes, nose and dock (see page 94). Throw up the loose edges of the rug at the back and brush the parts of the body exposed with the body brush. If they are stained, use the dampened water brush. Pull the rugs down again and give the pony his first feed of the day. Leave him to eat it and digest it in peace.

At about 9 o'clock or 9.30, return to the stable and remove any fresh droppings. The more often you do this, the more straw you will conserve as there will be less chance for the droppings to be trodden in and to get mixed up with the bedding. Now is the best time to give the pony his daily exercise, so remove the rugs and put on his tack. He should have a couple of hours of good exercise (Chapter two). On your return, spread the stacked-up bedding across the stable floor to give the pony a more comfortable place to stand, and refill the water bucket.

After his morning exercise the pony should receive a thorough grooming or 'strapping'. This is best done on return from work as the skin is warm and the dust and scurf will rise easily to the surface. Grooming is necessary to keep the horse healthy as well as looking clean and smart. Brushing massages the skin, stimulates the blood circulation, tones the muscles and generally helps to improve the horse's condition.

Begin by tying up the 'pony and

Remove all dirty and soiled bedding during the daily task of mucking-out.

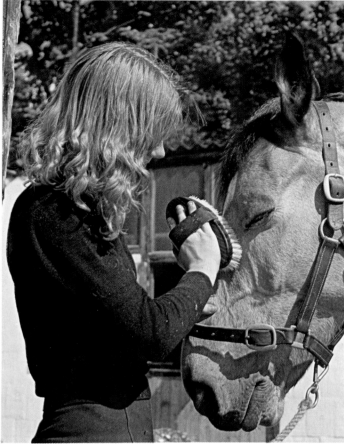

The first grooming of the day, called quartering (top left), entails brushing the parts of the coat exposed when the rugs are lifted. In the more thorough grooming, known as strapping, the head, body, legs, mane and tail are all brushed (above). Finally, the soles of the feet and the outer horn are oiled (bottom left).

picking out his feet again. If there is any caked mud or dried sweat marks on his body, brush these with the dandy brush. Brush the mane and tail with the body brush as explained on page 13. Now comes the hard work! Still using the body brush, brush the whole body starting from the top of the neck on one side and working towards the hindquarters. Then repeat this on the other side. Brush in short, firm circular strokes with the lay of the hairs, putting the brush firmly on to the body, but not banging it down. Hold the metal curry comb (a metal square with lines of serrated teeth across it) in the other hand and, after every three or four strokes, draw the body brush across it to remove the dust. The short bristles of the body brush are designed to reach right through to the skin, so they will pick up a lot of dust and scurf. Remove the dust from the curry comb by tapping it on the floor from time to time, but make sure you do this well away from the pony so that the dust does not merely fly back into his coat.

When you have completed brushing both sides of the body, brush the head gently. Now make a 'wisp' by twisting or plaiting together some strands of straw, dampen this slightly and use it all over the pony's body. The procedure now is to 'bang' it down gently on his coat, pulling it across in the direction of the hair growth. You will find it hard work – or you should do! It is, however, of great benefit to the pony in hardening his muscles, stimulating the flow of the blood to the skin and making his coat shine.

Sponge his eyes, nostrils and dock again, then gently brush the mane down with a dampened water brush so that it lies flat on one side of the neck. Wash his feet, if they are dusty or muddy, and oil them when they are dry. Add the final glossy touch to the coat by wiping all over the body with a stable rubber. Then replace the rugs for day wear and untie the pony. Refill the water bucket if necessary and give a second feed and a full hay net.

Bedding down

If your pony is having four feeds a day, he should be given his third feed between 4 o'clock and 4.30 in the afternoon. Any new droppings should be removed and the bed shaken to freshen it a little. If it is the cold season and already beginning to get dark by the middle of the afternoon, add whatever extra rugs or blankets you consider will be necessary for the night. Always leave a fresh bucket of water.

At about 7 o'clock in the evening, make the bed more comfortable in case your pony wants to lie down in the night. Once again, remove any fresh droppings and shake up the existing bedding. Add some new straw, tossing it to make sure it is well separated, and build up the sides of the bed around the stable walls. This will make it more comfortable for the pony as well as

making him less likely to hurt himself if he knocks against the sides of the box. He will also be better protected from any draughts when he lies down. Give him his final feed, some fresh water and a good, full, net of hay. Turn off the light and leave him in peace until the next morning.

The bored pony

It is important to remember that stabled horses and ponies may very easily get bored and boredom can often lead to the development of 'stable vices'. These include kicking the stable walls or door with front or hind legs, 'crib-biting' – which is gnawing at the top of the door or manger – 'weaving', when the pony stands, usually by the door, and sways rhythmically, from side to side, and windsucking, which involves arching the neck and gulping down air. The bored pony may even tear or chew at his rugs or begin to eat his bedding.

In all cases, try to ensure that such habits do not develop for, once established, they are hard to break. Leaving open the top part of the door of the stable, particularly if the box overlooks a busy yard, will help to relieve boredom, and so will your frequent visits. Crib-biting can be discouraged by painting the exposed surface with creosote, although this is not always successful. Muzzling the pony is one answer, but this is a drastic step to take. A stabled pony should not be made to wear a muzzle for long periods and never through the night. There are special collars available for the confirmed windsuckers. Make sure cribbiters and windsuckers always have supplies of hay – there is a chance that they might just nibble at that instead. All these vices will lead to an overall loss of condition and, in every case, prevention is better than cure, which, as already mentioned, is hard to achieve.

If kicking has already become an established habit, there is not a lot you can do about it. Try stepping up the amount of exercise if an excess of energy appears to be the cause. If you catch it

Stable vices include biting (top left) the door and constant rubbing of the neck (left). Many city parks have special bridle paths (right).

Riding on urban roads requires special care. Keep tucked well into the side at all times.

in its early stages you can deliver a sharp rap on the leg that is raised to strike. Do not think, however, that rough treatment will cure a confirmed kicker. It will probably make the situation worse and any treatment you mete out is likely to be repaid with interest.

Stabled horses and ponies must be given regular, daily exercise both to help relieve boredom and, more importantly, to keep them healthy and in good condition. Two hours' exercise a day is about the right amount to keep a stabled horse or pony really fit, which should include some hard trotting along a quiet road or track and some basic school work. Try to find a good, long, gradual incline that you can trot up, as part of the daily exercise. Trotting up and down hills helps to develop the animal's hindquarter muscles, to improve his balance and breathing and strengthen the lungs.

Do not ride over exactly the same route each day and, more particularly, if you do have to repeat many of the same roads and tracks, vary your changes of pace on each occasion. The exercise of a stabled pony may be part of a daily routine but it must never be allowed to become boring and mechanical for either of you.

In winter, if the ground is very hard and frosty and the roads slippery and icy, you can put a circle of straw in a field or paddock and drive, or 'lunge', the pony around this. 'Lunging' is extremely good exercise for a horse or pony and half an hour on the lunge is equivalent to being ridden for at least twice as long under normal circumstances. Remember to work evenly on both reins and to include some gentle cantering as well as trotting.

Always walk a sweating horse around gently for a time to allow him to cool off before returning him to the stable. If he is put back in the box while he is still hot and he is unable to walk round to cool off, he will soon become shivery. As a result he may catch cold and you will have even more work on your hands in nursing him back to health.

Do's and don'ts

Do ride on the same side as the on-going traffic and keep as close to the side of the road as possible, using grass verges if allowed.

Do observe road signs such as 'halt' or 'give way', traffic lights or control signals and police instructions.

Do give proper signals if you intend to slow down, turn to the left or right, or want to ask a motorist to stop.

Do be polite to motorists and thank those who slow down to pass you.

Do practise riding with the reins in one hand, thus leaving the other one free to signal. Keep your pony under complete control and attentive to your eishes at all times.

Do give way at pedestrian crossings and look both ways before moving off, turning or halting.

Do ride in single file if riding with others.

Don't ride out into a major road without stopping at the junction and looking right, left, then right again.

Don't canter along the road or grass verge. You should never ride faster than at a steady, controlled trot.

Don't ride on the road after dark unless completely unavoidable. If you have to ride in the dark, attach stirrup lamps to the irons and wear something light so that it will be reflected in the motorists' headlights.

Don't ride on a loose rein at any time and keep off roads altogether if they are particularly slippery.

Don't ride on mown grass in front of people's houses.

Don't look at any object that causes your pony to shy. Instead, turn his head away from it and keep driving him forward in a straight line.

Don't ride on the road at all unless you are completely confident you are going to be in full control under all circumstances.

4 The grass-kept pony

Some aspects of looking after ponies kept out at grass, catching them, turning out and grooming, for example, were discussed in Chapter one. Here we shall consider the overall care of a grass-kept animal in greater detail.

Whilst keeping a pony out-of-doors the year round and in a field is more 'natural' than keeping him stabled, he cannot be compared with the ponies who roam free over vast ranges of unfenced moorland or forest country. They can search far and wide for fresh grazing, water supplies and shelter, whereas the domestic pony kept in a confined space has only the facilities and resources offered him within that area. For this reason the grass-kept pony is totally dependent on man for his welfare and keep and, even though his needs are fewer than those of a stabled animal, he still requires daily care and attention.

Obvious advantages

There are obvious advantages in keeping horses or ponies 'turned out'. Much less time is taken up in looking after them and it is cheaper than keeping them stabled. Provided they are bred to withstand a variety of climatic conditions – and most horses and ponies are – they tend to be healthier than stabled animals. Ponies kept at grass are, by and large, also happier than their stabled counterparts. There is more in their immediate surroundings to occupy them and the problems of counteracting boredom are therefore not so great. However, they too appreciate company and most ponies appear to prefer to be turned out with other animals than to be on their own. This need not mean another pony. A great friendship may be struck up between a pony and a donkey, for example, and the peace of the countryside may be shattered by the raucous brays of the donkey every time his friend is taken off for a ride! Two or more ponies

LEFT: A small group of ponies graze contentedly on these rich and splendid pastures.

Churned-up conditions such as these are bad for ponies.

will generally get on well when turned out together, although on first acquaintance the opposite may appear to be true. Horses and ponies will often squeal and stamp their forefeet when they are first introduced in a field, but this does not mean that they will not get on in the future. It is best to leave them alone. They will soon settle their apparent differences. If one is notoriously difficult to catch, incidentally, he may well lead other field-mates into similarly bad habits. So be warned!

Finding a field and grazing can be quite a hard task if you do not own any land or if there is no suitable land near your house, and yet this is obviously your first consideration. The size of the field needed for a pony depends a little on the quality of the grass but, in any event, 0.8 hectares (2 acres) is really the

bare minimum for one animal. If you keep a pony in a smaller area, he will soon work his way through all the grazing and you will find that you have to supplement his diet with other food almost continuously.

Clean grazing

Horses and ponies are far fussier in their grazing habits than cattle, although they do not need the same rich grass as a cow expected to give a regular supply of milk. In fact, very rich pastures should be avoided, particularly for small ponies, as they will tend to over-gorge themselves – which can lead to all sorts of problems. Horses and ponies will only eat grass they like and will leave any that they have soiled with their own dung. This is one of the reasons why a pony should not be kept in the same field year in and year out. the pasture becomes 'horse-sick' and the risk of the animals getting worms

A wide, free opening along one side of this field shelter gives easy access for the ponies.

(see page 81) is greatly increased.

If you cannot find a second field where the pony can spend several months of the year, the field you have should be sectioned off. Each part of it should be rested in turn to give the new grass a chance to grow during the springtime. If a pony has access to the whole field at this time he is likely to damage much of its potential growth as he tramps over the ground to find the new and succulent patches. Also, if he is given access to vast quantities of rich, new grass, he will soon become excess-ively fat and correspondingly uneager to work.

Besides the quality of the grazing, any field you are considering as a potential home for your pony should be carefully examined to ensure that it contains no poisonous shrubs or plants. Those you are most likely to encounter are yew, ragwort, deadly nightshade and members of the hemlock family. These may be found growing anywhere in the field. If the field has a hedge on one or more sides, check this carefully to make sure no poisonous plants are growing half-hidden. Ragwort, deadly nightshade and hemlock can be elim-inated by pulling them up by the roots and burning them. Do not leave the dying branches in the field. Ponies seem to eat them even more greedily than the growing plant but it is at this time that they are at their most potent. Deal with yew either by chopping off all branches that are within reach or, better still, by fencing round the tree so the animal has no access to it.

Fencing

Your field must, of course, be fenced off, have a supply of fresh water and some form of shelter. The fencing must be strong, for no animal is more adept at blazing a trail to freedom through a flimsy barrier than a pony! Wooden posts and rails are the best, and most expensive, type of fencing. This lasts for

A line of trees down one side of the field offers natural protection.

years and is the type of fence least likely to cause injury to horses or ponies. However, unless it is there already it is often too expensive an item to install. The most usual alternative is a post with wire fencing, which is perfectly satisfactory and considerably cheaper, although not so long-lasting. If used, the wire must be really taut between the posts, and the bottom strand should be sufficiently high off the ground to discourage a pony from stepping over it in an attempt to reach greener grass on the other side. If he does this, he could start weakening the wire and may hurt himself as he pulls his leg back.

Hedges and walls are the other types of fencing most commonly encoun-tered. A thick hedge, which can also act as a windbreak, makes a good fence. A flimsy one is useless, for a pony will soon push his way through. Besides making sure the hedge contains no poisonous plants, remember it will also require occasional trimming and clipping.

The stone walls found in some areas make satisfactory boundaries, although if they are too low an active pony may be tempted to jump his way to freedom should something entice him from the other side. Again, they must always be kept in good repair.

Water supply

The one kind of fencing that should be avoided at all costs is barbed wire. Anyone who has seen the injury that barbed wire fencing can cause to horses or ponies will wholeheartedly agree. Electric fencing can be used, but really only has a value in sectioning-off part of a field when resting the grazing. It is not really satisfactory for the outer boundaries. If electric fencing is erected in a field where a pony is used to roaming the whole area, lead him to it and show it to him. He will soon get to realize what the ticking sound means and it might just prevent him from blundering into it, at the same time getting a shock and perhaps destroying the fencing.

Fencing of any kind should be checked regularly to ensure that no weaknesses are developing. Watch out for posts that are beginning to come loose in the ground, slack or trailing wires, bare patches developing in hedges, or stones becoming dislodged from the top of walls. Any such damage should be repaired without delay.

A gate must be, above all, strong and should latch securely without having to resort to loops of string or wire. It should swing freely on its hinges and be comfortably wide enough for you and your pony to pass through side-by-side. Five-bar gates, of either wooden or metal construction, are the best types. Make sure that the gate has a 'pony-proof' catch. Ponies can become amaz-ingly adept at undoing simple latches.

Some fields have a stream running through them from which a pony can drink whenever he is thirsty. More often, however, you will have to pro-vide some system to ensure there is a constant supply of fresh water. This will mean installing a trough of some kind. Make sure it has no sharp edges or the pony will suffer cuts and bruises to his knees each time he drinks. Old baths are best avoided for this reason, but they can be used if the sides are boxed-in in some way. The most effective way is to encase the sides in upright wooden planks that come level with the top of the bath. A continuous water supply is best provided by an automatic ball-cock arrangement in the tank, which should be covered over so that the pony cannot get at it. If the tank is left uncovered, he will find the ball-cock a great plaything and will soon ruin the workings. Remember to check the tank regularly. Falling leaves, dust and so on can soon affect the ball-cock's efficiency. And remember, too, that a water trough needs cleaning out at intervals of about every two months.

Providing shelter

Some sort of shelter must be provided for protection against wind, rain and cold or from the hot sun and troublesome flies in the summer. Even if the field is well supplied with mature shady trees, some sort of building is still desirable. Ideally, this should be a three-sided, brick or wooden shed with a well-insulated roof and a waterproof, non-slip floor. The open side, which should, if possible, face south allows the pony access at any time. Keep a thick layer of straw on the floor, so that the pony can lie down, although it is unlikely that he will do so very often. A loose box with a normal stable door, both parts of which are kept permanently open, is not very satisfactory. Two or more ponies turned out in the field may both want to go inside at the same time. If one tends to bully the other, they could injure themselves by not being able to get out of the stable quickly enough if a squabble develops or by getting squeezed together as they make a rush for the door. It is much better to have an entirely open side to a field shelter.

Do not be surprised if you find the shelter really coming into its own and getting the most use from the pony in the summer. It offers a welcome escape from flies, which tend to be more of an irritant to ponies than the very worst weather conditions.

Daily inspection of the field is necessary both to check the fencing, as already mentioned, and to make sure that no broken bottles or other 'hazards' have been thrown in over the fence by thoughtless people. By removing the pony's droppings each day, you do much to conserve and extend the grazing as well as lessen the chances of a pony suffering an attack of worms. Horses and ponies generally have some worms in their gut and the eggs and larvae are passed out in their dung. If these are allowed to remain in the field they will soon hatch and multiply, and the chances of the pony picking them up as he grazes will be increased. Having the field grazed by cattle from time to time – they will eat the infected grass without suffering any ill effects –

Keep a constant look out around the field for harmful rubbish which may have been thrown in.

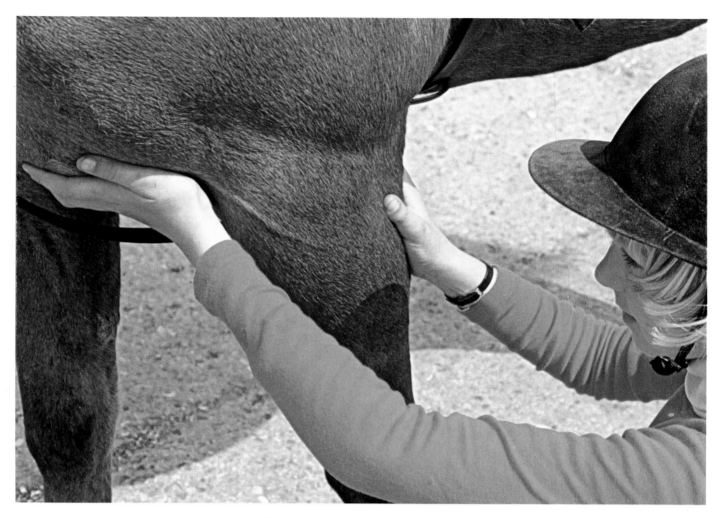

Check the pony's legs and body each day to make sure he has not sustained any injuries.

and resting parts of the field in rotation are other ways to lessen the likelihood of infection.

To keep the grazing as healthy as possible, seek the advice of an expert on such matters, such as a local farmer. All grassland needs periodic cutting, harrowing and reseeding if it is to remain in permanent good condition and a farmer should be able to give on-the-spot advice for your particular field.

Ponies kept at grass must be visited every day to make sure they are still there and that they have not hurt themselves during the preceding night. Get into the habit of catching up your pony when you visit him each day. Run your hands over his body and legs to feel for any small cuts, lumps or bumps, and pick out his feet in case any stones have become lodged and are causing him discomfort. Make a fuss of him

before turning him out again, so that he associates your visit with pleasure.

However much care you take to conserve the pasture and to keep it in good condition and however healthy your pony may be, he will always have some parasitic worms in his gut. These will do little harm but, if allowed to multiply, they will affect the pony's overall physical condition. He will become thin and permanently hungry and his coat will lose any gloss or shine. However much extra food you give him, he will not put on weight. For this reason, all horses and ponies, especially those kept at grass, should be wormed once a year or once in the spring and again in the late autumn. This involves giving a dose of an anti-worm drug, usually in the form of a powder which is mixed in with the feed. As with all medical preparations, new types of drugs are continually coming on to the market, so always seek the advice of your veterinary surgeon to see what type he recommends.

Various types of parasitic worm thrive in horses and ponies, the most dangerous being the red worm. This attacks the lining of the gut and bowel and serious infestation can lead to recurring bouts of colic throughout an animal's life. In really severe cases it can lead to death. Red worms will always attack weakened animals, and young horses and ponies (those under five years old) are generally more vulnerable than older ones who have built up a greater natural resistance. If your pony is a youngster, watch particularly for any signs of weakness, emaciation or an apparent proneness to ill health, any of which could be a sign of worms.

Supplementary feeding

Ponies kept at grass all the year round will need their diet supplemented by additional food at various times. As we already know, the grass begins to grow in early spring. It is at its best from late spring to early summer and by mid-autumn it ceases all growth until

Stay with the pony when you feed him if there are other ponies in the field who may steal his food.

the following spring. Generally there is sufficient grazing to sustain a pony throughout the spring and summer, but by autumn and winter he will need additional food to supply both bulk and nutriment.

Supplementary feeding may also be necessary in the summer, too – a fact that is often overlooked. In a very hot sunny summer, the grazing will soon become 'burnt-out' and deprived of goodness.

Ponies graze mostly in the daylight hours. Little serious eating is done after dark. The most concentrated times are, in fact, the early daylight hours and, for

a time, before dusk sets in. In the winter, therefore, when it begins to get dark in the mid-afternoon, a pony has less time to fill himself with the bulk he needs to maintain his physical condition. You should therefore make sure that grass-kept ponies have a constant and adequate supply of hay. Bulk food in the form of hay is as important as nutritional foodstuffs in keeping a pony healthy. Deprived of the bulk, he will soon lose the fat accumulated through the spring and summer and weight lost in the winter is almost impossible to put back until the following spring. On the other hand, a good layer of fat is necessary for keeping a pony insulated and warm.

The same principles of feeding hay to stabled horses and ponies apply in the case of those kept at grass. Feed only the best possible hay, make sure that it is not musty, dusty or mouldy and give it in a hay net. If you put hay directly on to the ground in a field, much will be wasted since the pony will inevitably trample it into the ground. A hay net can be tied to a stout branch of a tree or you can have a ring put in the wall of the shelter at a suitable height and tie the haynet to this. Avoid hooking it over or tying it to a fence post. As the pony tugs at the strands of hay he will, in time, undermine and weaken the post's stronghold in the ground.

Begin supplementary feeding by giving a full hay net in the afternoon. Then, as the days get shorter and winter draws on, increase this to two hay nets a day, crammed as full as you can get them. Put them out to correspond with the pony's time of intense grazing – that is, as we already know, early morning and an hour or so before it begins to get dark.

'Short' feeds

Most ponies, especially those expected to do a lot of work, will need additional concentrated food. Such feeds, consisting of corn or grain, are known as 'short' feeds. The same basic foodstuffs given to stabled ponies will be used.

The best type of short feed for a pony at grass is pony cubes, ideally mixed with dampened bran. Oats, flaked maize or beans are all foodstuffs that tend to heat up and excite ponies. It is particularly unwise to use them for ponies that are receiving irregular exercise, which is often the case with grass-kept ponies. Pony cubes will provide all the nutriments and vitamins a pony needs without making him over-excitable.

Once you have begun to give short feeds, perhaps in the late autumn, you must continue to do so regularly each day until the new grass begins to come through. Do not fall into the trap of giving a feed only if you intend to ride the pony the next day. It will do him no good, nor is it fair to give him odd feeds just now and then. He will begin to expect a feed at a certain time and will not understand why one is not forthcoming. It certainly will not improve his mood when you go to see him.

One short feed a day from mid-winter to early spring will probably be sufficient for most grass-kept ponies being ridden mainly at weekends, provided they have begun the winter in good condition. Do not stop giving feeds too early in the spring. Most ponies lose condition gradually through the winter and are at their lowest ebb as spring breaks through.

Keeping food

Care must be taken when feeding grass-kept ponies if two or more are turned out together. Friendship quickly turns to enmity when food appears. Put down the feeds well apart and stay to make sure that one pony does not gobble his in double-quick time so he can move in on his friend's. If only one pony is receiving supplementary feeding, either take the animal out of the field and well out of sight to have his feed so that the others are not envious, or give them a 'fake' meal consisting mainly of bran, perhaps with just a handful of nuts added to make the bran more appetizing. When several ponies are turned out together, it is even more important to keep to the same time of feeding each day. If they are kept waiting for their feed, they will soon get cross with one another and fighting may well break out.

Keep your pony's feed in a dry and clean place, ideally in a lock-up shed or barn. Large dustbins, either of galvanized iron or strong rubber, make ideal food containers and are generally more rat-proof than open bins. Always measure feeds out carefully to ensure you give the same amount each day and remember that nothing is really to be gained by giving an extra handful of nuts or oats before or after a hard day's work.

As in feeding hay, it is wasteful to put a short feed on the ground since much will be lost under the hungry pony's hooves. It should be put in a container – either a strong box or special food bin

Tie the hay net (above right) by looping the drawn-up end back through the side of the net. Use a quick release knot. RIGHT: Make sure the haynet in the field is positioned at the right height for the pony to eat from.

that is placed on to the ground or, if your pony is the type that likes to tip the food out of the box, a food bin that hooks on to a fence may be the answer. You can only hook these on to wooden posts and rails, however, not over a strand of wire.

Hay should be stored in dry conditions and preferably close to the field, so that you do not have to transport heavy bales from very far away. There should be plenty of ventilation in the building as it is important that air should circulate around bales of hay. If the ground is at all damp, protect the hay by putting a covering of straw bales underneath, so that it is not in direct contact with the ground.

Changing needs

Always remember that the needs of the grass-kept pony will change with the seasons. Winter conditions, for example, call for extra thought on your part to ensure the pony is not suffering from the cold. If the temperature drops to below freezing, it will be necessary to break the ice on the water trough. Drinking icy water will do the pony no harm, but he is generally unable to break the ice by himself to get to the water underneath. If it is freezing through the day, it may even be necessary to break the ice three times – in the early morning, at midday and again in the late afternoon.

When the ground becomes very hard owing to heavy frosts or if is covered with a layer of snow, you will have to increase the hay ration as there will be no grazing for the pony to nibble at. Do not stop giving the extra rations as soon as the snow disappears for the grass that is there will be soggy and unappetizing.

Most ponies grow thick long coats to see them through the winter. When the weather is very cold, you will notice that the hairs of the coat stand up on end. This has the effect of trapping a layer of warm air inside the coat, thus giving additional insulation. As discussed in Chapter one, the natural grease in the coat also acts as an insulator and helps to repel the rain.

If for some reason a pony does not grow a sufficiently thick coat to protect him against the worst of the weather conditions – either because he is more highly bred than the native types (see

Chapter eight) or because he was stabled in the early autumn so that his winter coat did not have a chance to grow fully, it may be necessary to provide him with clothing for additional warmth. The only rug that is suitable for outdoor conditions is the New Zealand rug. This is made of strong, waterproof and windproof material lined with wool. In addition to the chest buckle and surcingle to keep it in place, it has two leather straps attached to the sides. These are taken between the pony's hindlegs and clipped in place. They halp to prevent the back of the rug slipping from the side.

New Zealand rugs are extremely useful items of clothing for grass-kept ponies, but do not imagine that you can just put one on your pony and then forget about it. The rug must be removed every day and the pony's hair smoothed over with your hands before replacing the rug. If you do not do this, it is probable that the rug will start to rub him at various points, which may go undetected, and bare patches right down to his skin could develop. He will then not be able to go on wearing the rug, because it is rubbing him raw, and yet you cannot turn him out in the field with no protective clothing. Prevention is the obvious answer to this problem. Keep the leather leg straps well oiled so they are soft and supple. Rain and mud will soon make them hard and they will begin to rub bare patches on the animal's hind legs. If this does happen, try encasing the straps in rubber tubing (using an inner tube from a bicycle tyre) or sheepskin. At the same time as keeping the straps supple and free from caked mud, make sure you brush off any mud from the pony's legs at the places where the straps rest, for this will have the same abrasive effect.

Bad weather

If you have been riding in the rain, dry the pony by putting straw over his back under a piece of sacking (see page 13) before replacing the New Zealand rug. Never put the rug on a soaking wet pony. He will be extremely uncomfortable as his coat begins to dry out and it will get very hot and clammy under the rug. Never ride a pony wearing a New Zealand rug or stand him in the stable wearing it. Because it

Ponies will come to no harm in frosty or snowy conditions if they have a good thick coat and enough extra food to supplement their diet. RIGHT: An ideal water trough for a field or paddock. There are no sharp edges and the ballcock mechanism is completely enclosed. FAR RIGHT: This rug, known as a New Zealand rug, is the only type of rug suitable for ponies turned out to grass.

is waterproof, it allows no air through to the skin and this will again cause him discomfort.

Always watch out for bruised feet and soles in winter-time, especially if the ground is very hard and frosty. Make sure the pony is shod properly, even if you are not riding him a great deal. Shoeing will help to protect the

horn of the hoof from becoming cracked, as will keeping the hoof well oiled. Rubbing grease into the back of the heels will help to guard against a condition known as 'cracked, heels', which can develop in cold or wet weather. If you have a very wet winter and if the ground in your field does not drain well so that the land becomes excessively muddy, the pony can develop 'mud fever'. Seek the advice of your veterinary surgeon for treatment but try to guard against its occurrence by fencing off any really muddy areas.

Summer time

Looking after a grass-kept pony in summer time is easier than in winter, but there are still points to bear in mind. Remember to keep a watchful eye on the grazing in excessively hot, dry weather in case it becomes burnt-out. You will easily recognize this be-

TOP LEFT: Swarms of buzzing flies are among the greatest plagues for grass-kept ponies. LEFT: This summer sheet is made of cotton and keeps the dust off a newly-groomed pony.

cause the grass turns yellow or brown and the ground, too, is likely to become cracked and very dry and dusty.

The biggest irritation to a pony in hot weather is flies. They will plague him unmercifully, buzzing in his eyes and nostrils. Two ponies turned out together will help one another by standing for hours on end, head-to-tail, swishing the flies away from the other's face. The fly problem is yet another vicious circle. The pony will want to stand in the shade of a tree to escape the glare and heat of the sun, but that is where the worst swarms of flies are to be found. Thus the distraught pony is driven out into the sun again to escape them. The field shelter probably offers better protection from flies than the shade of the trees, and is important for this reason. You will find the pony spends more time inside it in the summer than in the winter. Various anti-fly lotions and spray repellents are marketed, but none are really effective. The fly net, which is a fringed arrangement attached to the headstrap of a headcollar to come down over the face, can sometimes be a help, but it is more often used for ponies that are tethered,

With lush pastures (left) a supplementary feed is not required as in the case of parched grass.

perhaps between events at a summer show, than for those turned out in a field.

Grass-kept horses and ponies can lose condition quite considerably because of flies. The animal's urge to get rid of them by stamping his hooves and shaking his head may be stronger than the urge to eat or, as often happens, he may walk endlessly around the field in an effort to be one step ahead of the buzzing swarms. When horses get really frustrated by the problem, they will shake their heads, kick up their heels and take off at a mad gallop, without realizing that their escape is only temporary.

In very hot weather you should, of course, ensure that the water supply remains in good working order. If there is a lot of dust flying about in the air, it might, as we already know, affect the ball-cock system, stopping it from operating efficiently. The water level would then drop and the supply dry out altogether without you noticing it.

This anti-sweat rug is most commonly worn by racehorses to prevent chills after a race.

If you do not want to keep a pony constantly stabled, and yet do not want to turn him out to grass for the entire year, there is another alternative and that is to keep him on a half-and-half or combined system. This way he is turned out in the field for part of the day and brought in for the other part. Keeping a pony like this has a number of advantages and can combine the best of both systems for you and for the pony. He will remain fitter and cleaner than if he is permanently out in the field and yet he is not completely deprived of the more natural outdoor life. The work involved for you comes mid-way between the two systems: more work than for a totally grass-kept pony, but less than for a full-time stabled animal.

If this kind of system is adopted, the most usual arrangement is to turn the pony out by day in the winter, bringing him in at night, and to reverse the proceedings in the summer. In the winter, he will not then have to brave the cold wintry nights, but he will need to be turned out in a New Zealand rug during the day and he will probably be a little less 'hardy' than other ponies kept out all the time. It means, too, that you could have his coat partially clipped (see page 67) if you like. This will assist in maintaining a neater appearance and it will also keep him fitter as

he will not get so hot when asked to work hard. A pony kept this way will need more concentrated food and hay than one turned out all the time, but it will not be necessary to give the thorough daily strapping (see page 68) or to take him out on exercise each day.

Bringing a pony into the stable during the day in the summer helps to relieve him of the irritation of flies and also means he is immediately available for you to ride. You can regulate the amount of grass he eats, which is important if the grass is very lush and the pony very greedy. On the other hand, if the pony is not over-fat, give him a small net of hay in the middle of the day as he stands in the stable. He will have something to nibble at and it will relieve his boredom. The most usual timing is to bring a pony into the stable around 10 o'clock in the morning and turn him back out again at about 5 o'clock in the afternoon. This way he is not robbed of his most concentrated grazing period at either end of the day.

Part-time stabling

In the summer, part-time stabling can be provided by the field shelter, so long as it is big enough for the pony to turn around and lie down comfortably. Just suspend a couple of poles across the open side to keep him inside and put a layer of bedding on the floor. Even if the pony does not want to lie down, it will be uncomfortable for him to stand on a bare floor all day. Make sure, of

course, there is a constant supply of fresh water. When you turn the pony out in the evening, remove any droppings or soiled bedding and prepare the stable for the following day.

Stabling for a pony that is going to be brought in at nights in the winter should be of the more conventional type with a normal two-part door and a window. As usual, leave the top part of the door open, providing any extra warmth that may be necessary with rugs rather than by shutting the door. The pony will require a thick bed similar to that provided for a pony kept full-time in the stable, which will have to be properly mucked-out each morning after you have turned him out in the field for the day. Give him his morning feed in the stable before turning him out.

If the pony is wet when you bring him in at night, dry him off in the way described on page 13. Do not leave him to stand in the stable in his wet state.

Riding etiquette

Keeping a pony out at grass all the year does not mean that you have to be living in the country. However, this will probably be the case since urban surroundings do not generally offer much in the way of grazing land. But it will mean that you are likely to be keeping your pony for leisure hacking rather than for competitive purposes, for which he would need the fitness that comes with stabling and hard regular exercise. Such hacking is usually done across pasture and woodland rather than along the road.

The rules outlined for riding on roads in towns on page 75 apply equally to riding on the roads in more rural areas. Almost wherever you go for a ride you will have to ride along some roads. There are, in addition, some other points to bear in mind when riding in the countryside and across farm land. Remember, your behaviour when you are out for a ride can affect the reputation of the riding community as a whole. It may also make all the difference as to whether a farmer allows riders over his land or not.

First of all, make sure that you shut all gates securely behind you, particularly if the field you have just left or entered has cattle, sheep or other livestock grazing in it. Never ride fast through fields where other animals are grazing. You could well incite them to riot if you go tearing across the land and this could cause untold damage if it is close to lambing or calving time. The best procedure is to ride quietly round the edge of the field at a steady walk.

If a field is sown or ploughed, again

keep to the outside edge and ride as close to the fence as possible. When you are riding with others, keep in single file. Never ride across a crop of wheat or grain at any stage of its growth. You will damage it irreparably. Similarly, if the ground is very muddy or marshy from constant rain, keep to the outside of all fields, whether they are sown or not. Horses' and ponies' hooves can churn up soft ground quicker than anything.

Do not jump hedges or fences that

separate fields. Should you accidentally crash through one, you will have ruined good fencing, which is not only expensive to repair but also serves as an enclosure for animals who would otherwise be free to wander off.

On tracks and bridle paths through woods, show due consideration to any pedestrians enjoying a quiet stroll in the country. Slow down to go past them at a walk – never faster. It can be very frightening to have a pony thunder past you when you are on foot. Remember

This pony has been trace clipped. His winter coat has been clipped from his belly and under his neck.

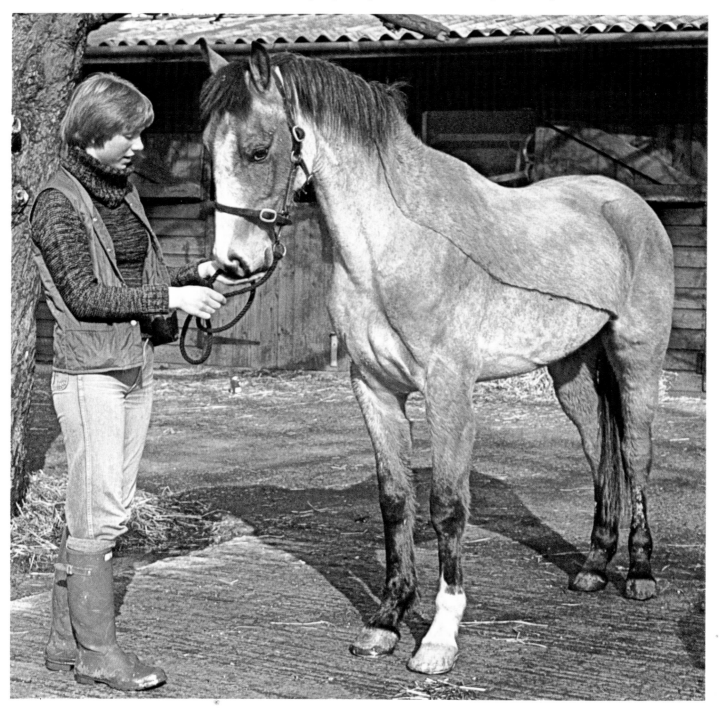

to thank them if they have stepped off the path to let you by, which they are likely to have done. Similarly, if riding across a common or park which has no set bridle paths or tracks for you to follow, consider pedestrians and do not ride in such a way that you are not able to stop instantly or are in danger of losing control. Commons and park land are not places to test your pony's speed against a friend's in a madcap race.

Think of others

Whenever you are riding with others, temper the speed of the ride to the capabilities and standard of the least experienced or novice rider. It is simply not fair to ask people to ride faster than they want to or to jump obstacles that they feel are too big for them. If someone falls off on a ride (and it could be you next time), wait for them to get back to their feet and remount, catching the pony for them if necessary. And if a pony does take it into his head to bolt with his rider, never chase after them in hot pursuit. This will just urge the pony even faster, for he will think he is being challenged to a race. Instead, try to head him off by cutting across his path at an angle. If it is your pony that is bolting, try just to sit still quietly and not panic. Drop the reins loosely round his neck. There is no point in pulling against him at this stage, for he will obviously be deaf to the command.

If at any time you find yourself riding across a field or in a wood where the ground is very uneven – maybe scattered with large stones or pitted with rabbit holes – the best thing to do is to ride on a loose rein, letting the pony stretch his neck forward. This way he can see the ground better and you will find he is much cleverer at picking his way safely through the obstacles than you are at guiding him.

Remember, at all times let your common sense prevail in telling you what to do. You will find this is generally the best guide.

Always shut gates (top left) behind you when out for a ride. Keep well into the edge of a field of crops (left) and lean forward (right) when you ride beneath low-hanging branches to avoid banging your head or being swept off the pony.

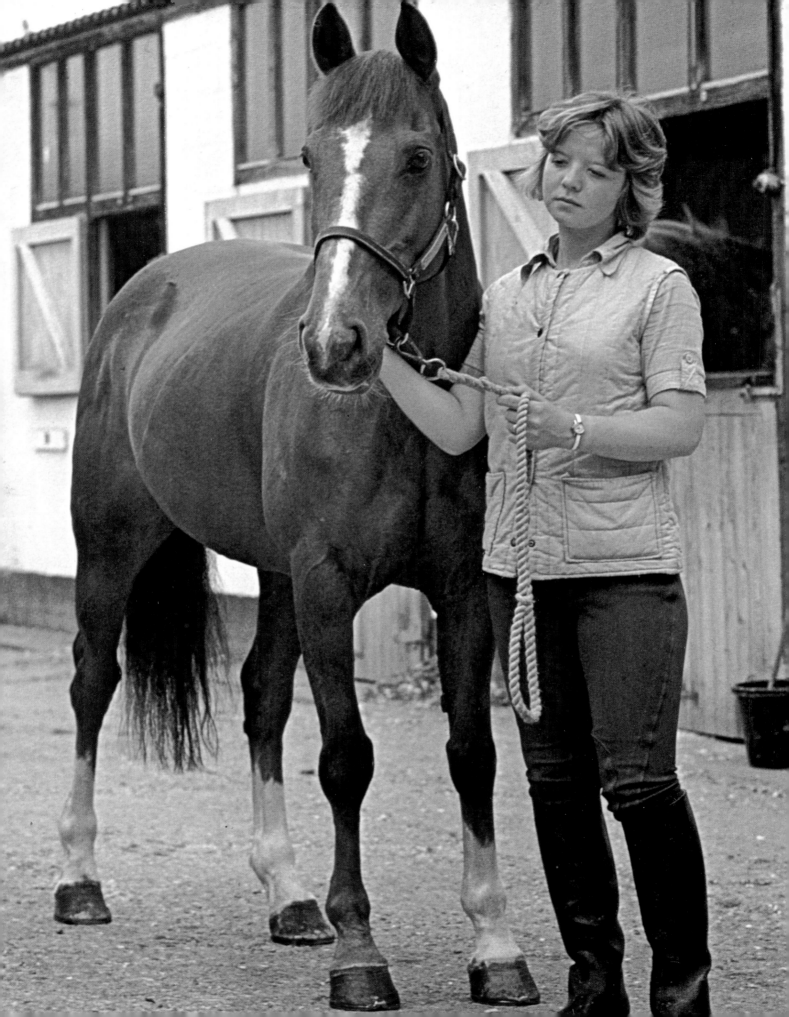

5 Your pony's health

All horsemen and horsewomen must be able to recognize if their horse or pony is feeling off-colour. Horses and ponies are as much subject to illness, disease and injury as any animal, and any such affliction, however minor, means they are unlikely to give of their best. Furthermore, if a pony is worked hard when he is not feeling in peak health, this could lead to a considerable worsening of his condition.

Observing behaviour

There are signs that can tell us whether a horse or pony is healthy and in good condition, but we must remember that every horse or pony is an individual and will both look and behave like an individual. You can learn to recognize the indications that your pony is healthy and happy by observing his behaviour when he is grazing, feeding, drinking or resting in his field or stable, as well as when you are riding him.

A healthy horse or pony will normally be alert and interested in what is going on around him. This does not mean he is constantly jittery and looking nervously all about him but that he takes notice of his surroundings and registers anything unusual. His ears will flicker backwards and forwards, picking up new sounds even when he is grazing quietly or resting. The eyes should look bright and there should be no discharge from them or from his nostrils. The coat will be generally smooth, glossy and even in thickness with no bald or thinning patches, which might be caused by rubbing due to a skin irritation. He should stand evenly on all four legs, although if he does rest a hind leg from time to time there need be no great cause for concern. If he rests or points a forefoot, this is often an indication that the forefoot is tender or is causing him some pain. He should breathe easily and regularly although, after a bout of excessive exer-

This pony has been carefully fed, exercised and groomed over three months to improve his condition.

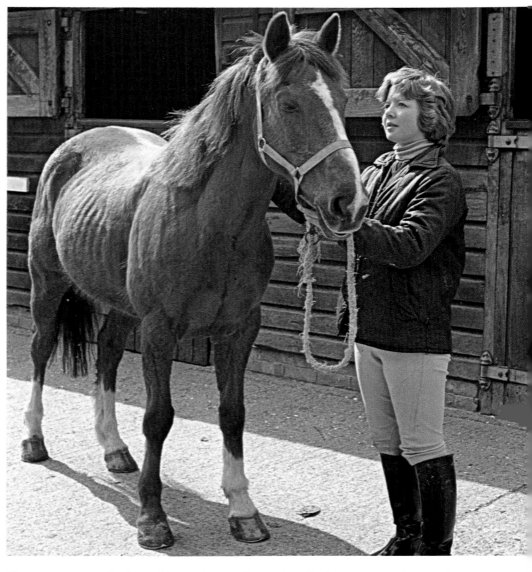

The same pony, looking thin and scruffy, before undergoing a well-maintained stable routine.

tion during a ride, he will probably puff and pant a little, particularly if he is not completely fit. He should not appear unduly cold or hot at any time and should not shiver or break into a sweat for no apparent reason.

Appetite is a good clue to a horse or pony's state of health, for they are nearly always voracious feeders. If an animal shows no interest in a feed when it is put out for him, this is certainly a matter of investigation. Although there should be a good layer of flesh covering a horse's rib cage, remember that it is

just as bad for him to be too fat as to be too thin. A fat pony is likely to be out of condition and he could soon develop problems if he is ridden too hard. His respiratory system could suffer and he is more likely to strain a tendon or ligament in his legs.

Points of a horse

Knowing the correct names for the various parts, or points, of a horse is essential so that you can identify them by name if you need to describe an abnormality to a veterinary surgeon. The main points are shown on our annotated illustration overleaf.

Paying attention to a horse or pony's feet, although not directly related to his

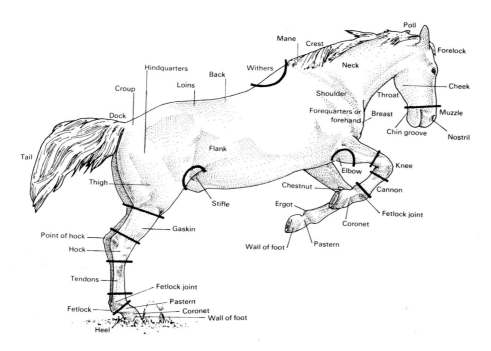

It is important to know the basic structure of the horse and the names given to the various parts.

general health, is still an important aspect of maintaining his overall condition. Lameness puts a working horse out of action and the foot is often a cause of lameness. Ponies wandering 'wild' across open country keep their feet in good condition naturally. The constant roaming to find new grazing keeps the horn from growing too long and the absence of being ridden along roads or hard tracks at a fast pace means that the foot does not wear down too much. The feet of a domestic pony turned out in a field will soon grow too long from lack of exercise or, if he is being ridden, iron shoes must be fitted to ensure that the horn does not wear down to such an extent that the sensitive parts of the feet become exposed and start causing pain. The blacksmith or farrier is an extremely important person to any owner of a horse of pony.

The other person who is vital in ensuring your pony's good health is the veterinary surgeon. As soon as you acquire a horse or pony, you must 'acquire' a veterinary surgeon, for there will inevitably be occasions when you need to seek his advice and professional expertise. Keep his telephone number displayed in a prominent position such as the wall of the tack room or next to the telephone. Obviously you should be

guided by common sense and discretion in deciding whether to call in the vet, but as a general rule it is better to call him and be safe rather than be sorry. Before you do ring him, take a careful note of all the symptoms or signs that have led you to seek his advice, so that you can clearly describe these to him on the telephone. He may be able to tell you what course of action or treatment to take without coming to see the pony. If not, at least he has some knowledge of what to expect when he arrives.

Your horse or pony is likely to suffer all manner of minor complaints and various odd cuts and injuries that you can attend to without calling in the vet, provided you have reasonable First Aid facilities. You must also know and follow the basic rules for applying First Aid, which are largely dictated by common sense.

First Aid

The First Aid equipment – and this should be kept together in one place – includes a clean bowl or bucket, cotton wool or gamgee tissue, lint, bandages about 7.5 cm (3 in) wide for cuts and wounds, blunt-ended scissors, a clinical thermometer, a tin of kaolin paste, antiseptic solution and cream, antibiotic wound powder, a cough electuary and one or two colic drinks. The wound powder, cough electuary and colic drinks should all be obtained from your veterinary surgeon since new

brands are continually appearing on the market. It is unlikely that you will personally administer some of the items in your First Aid equipment, such as the thermometer, the cough electuary and colic drinks, at least not without professional advice or assistance. Nevertheless, they should still be there and should be available if needed.

All First Aid provisions should be kept in a clean, hygienic place away from the dirt and dust inevitably created near or in a stable. Preferably they should be kept under lock and key in their own cupboard. When applying First Aid for any reason, the first rule is to get someone to hold the animal by the bridle or headcollar. Do not attempt to treat an injured horse or pony while he is free in the stable or tied up by the headcollar rope. Both situations could be dangerous. The treatment you give might cause temporary pain, making the animal jump and kick out or pull back violently.

Calling the vet

Always wash your hands before attending to an injury, particularly if you are dealing with an open wound. It goes almost without saying that you should use only clean, preferably sterilized or disinfected equipment, whether bowls, swabs or dressings. Talk quietly to the pony as you treat him so as to calm and reassure him and work as gently, but as quickly, as you can. Make sure you follow accurately any instructions given on medical preparations.

If you are making the animal comfortable before the veterinary surgeon's arrival or cleaning a wound to assess whether it is necessary to call the vet, do as little as possible. Leave all the major treatment to the vet. Once you have decided that it is necessary to call the vet do so as quickly and calmly as you can, preferably leaving the animal in some responsible person's charge while you go to telephone. If no one is around, leave the horse or pony in the stable and tie him up if you feel he should be kept still.

When a veterinary surgeon is examining a horse or pony, he will probably want you to hold the animal for him. You should stand in front of the pony and hold the sides of the headcollar in either hand, talking quietly to him all the time. If the vet is examining a painful hind leg, he may want you to hold up a front leg as this makes it almost impossible for the pony to kick out. Always follow carefully the vet's instructions for further treatment. Never think that you know better and try some other course of action.

Among the most common ailments you are likely to have to deal with as a pony owner is a cough or cold. Just like people, ponies contract coughs and colds either if they are in contact with other infected animals or if they are kept in cold, draughty conditions for long periods. Cold symptoms are a discharge from the nose and eyes, general listlessness and maybe shivering

RIGHT: This horse has been put under sedation and tied up before undergoing a minor operation.
BELOW: The Vet's assistant makes sure the horse remains unconscious throughout the operation.

in extreme cases. The cold will sometimes be accompanied by a cough but a pony can develop a cough without having a cold. Eating dusty hay is a frequent cause.

If your pony has a cough or cold, stop working him at once. If you ride him hard at this time, particularly if he has a cough, you could permanently damage his breathing by bringing on a condition known as 'broken wind'. He will then have a constant deep cough which will be with him for ever and you will never be able to ride him hard or enter him in competitions. A pony with a cough or cold should be kept warm in an airy, draught-free stable and isolated from other ponies to reduce the risk of the infection spreading. Cut down his food rations and give him light, laxative feeds, such as gruels or bran mashes with lots of fresh succulent green food or root vegetables. For a bad cough a veterinary surgeon may recommend regular doses of a cough electuary. This is administered by placing a small amount on the back of the animal's tongue and holding up his head until he swallows. Your vet will show you how to do this.

Infectious diseases

Horses and ponies are also subject to equine influenza, the symptoms of which are similar to those of a bad cold but are generally rather more pronounced. Treatment follows the same lines: rest from any work, a light diet and isolation in an airy, draught-free stable. Isolation is most important when an animal has influenza since this is among the most infectious of all diseases and will soon affect an entire stable. Horses and ponies can be immunized against equine 'flu by a course of injections and if you have any reason to suppose your pony may come into contact with the condition, you would be wise to consult your vet about protecting him in this way.

Another disease which demands instant isolation is 'strangles'. In some ways this is akin to glandular fever in humans and it generally attacks young horses and ponies. Older ones seem to build up a natural immunity. The disease is characterized by the swelling of the glands on either side of the throat and a heavy discharge from the nostrils. These symptoms are usually accompanied by a high temperature denoting the fever, a noticeable loss of appetite and a generally uncomfortable appearance and unhappy demeanour. Prompt treatment is essential. A veterinary surgeon will prescribe suitable drugs and explain what action you should take. You will be advised to isolate the animal as already mentioned, keeping him warm, comfortable and quiet in a draught-free stable with a good, thick bed of straw. All equipment used for a pony with strangles should be kept frequently disinfected and used solely

An anti-tetanus injection is being given to safeguard against a bad cut the pony has sustained.

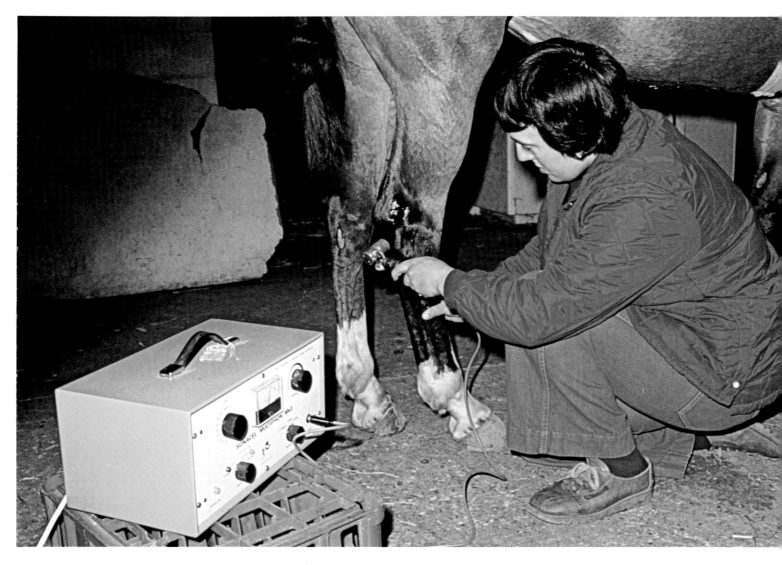

Ultrasonic radiation waves are applied to the pony's leg to help to reduce a swelling.

for him. When he has recovered from the disease, it must all be sterilized if it is to be put back into general use. The stable, too, should be cleaned and thoroughly disinfected.

The condition known as colic has already been mentioned several times. In effect, colic is severe indigestion with very bad tummy ache. But it is generally a more serious complaint than indigestion in humans and in really severe cases can lead to an animal's death.

The symptoms of colic are unmistakable. Your pony will probably break out in a sweat, paw the ground and try to bite his belly or strike at it with one of his hind legs. Obvious discomfort may make him wander around fretfully,

unable to settle, and he may also try to get down and roll on the floor.

Your first course of action is to call in the veterinary surgeon. However, it is important not to let the pony roll, for his energetic writhings can lead to a 'twisted gut'. This is quite literally a twist or knot occurring in the intestines, which will cause death. Either get someone to hold the animal while you call the vet or, if you are on your own, tie him up on a short rope in the stable. You can also prevent him from rolling by walking him about, which is a good thing to do unless he is already completely exhausted. If he is very cold and shivery, put a rug on him to try and make him warmer.

Attacks of colic vary greatly in intensity. Some last about an hour or so and cause only mild discomfort rather than acute pain, while others can last for a considerable time. A veterinary

surgeon will usually administer a colic drink which helps to relieve the condition.

Colic is caused by a number of things, most of which we have already mentioned. Among the most common of these are giving poor feed, making sudden changes in the diet and heavy riding immediately after a large feed, before there has been sufficient time for digestion. If your pony seems liable to colic, try to find out the cause and make sure you avoid it in the future.

Common sense

The nursing of sick horses and ponies is another aspect of horsemanship that is best governed by common sense. When you are dealing with a sick or distressed animal try not to become irrational or over anxious. The first requirement is to make the patient as comfortable as possible. If he is used to

This horse has just undergone an operation. The box is thickly padded round the sides and floor to prevent him from hurting himself when he comes round and tries to stand.

being with others, try to keep him in a place where he can at least see all his companions, unless he is so infectious that he must be kept in complete isolation.

Depending on the nature of the complaint, a small paddock may make better 'sick quarters' for a sick pony than the stable, particularly if the weather is mild. Nature's cures of healthy fresh air and clean grazing are often more effective than manufactured medical preparations. If it is necessary to keep a horse stabled, ensure that the building is totally free from draughts but has adequate ventilation and is

light and airy. Put a good thick bed of straw on the floor and keep this clean and fresh at all times. Make sure all feed bowls and water buckets are kept spotlessly clean and, if your pony has a bad cold with a heavy nasal discharge, renew the water supply frequently.

When a pony has suffered from an infectious illness, disinfect his stable and all the equipment used during the isolation period. This includes any rugs and bandages he may have worn.

The odd injury

There are, of course, numerous diseases a pony owner or handler may encounter. Obviously, we cannot discuss them all in detail here, so once again be guided by common sense whenever you discover or notice something unusual about your pony's general condition. If you are ever in any

doubt about why your pony is off-colour or not quite up to the mark, call your veterinary surgeon.

Besides the various diseases and ailments to which horses and ponies are prone, you must be prepared for the fact that your pony will collect odd minor injuries during the course of your time together. The nature of a domestic horse or pony's existence – being ridden across country, asked to jump various obstacles and so on – means that he will inevitably suffer minor cuts, tears and bruises. Most of these will not be serious and you will be able to treat them yourself quite easily.

Wounds can be grouped into four

Mare and foal. It is advisable to inform your vet when birth is due although he may not be needed.

98

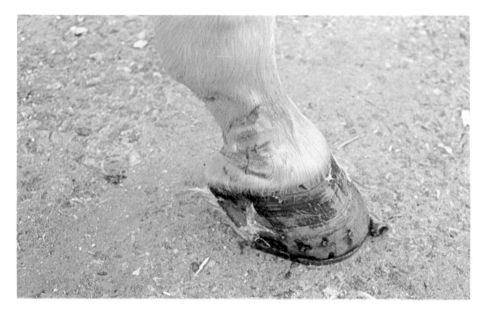

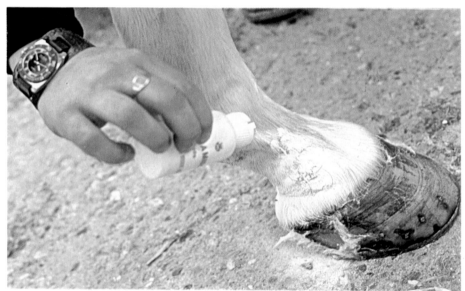

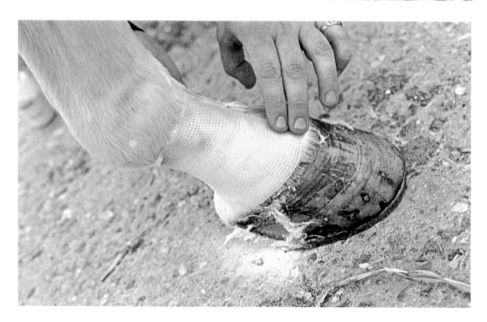

categories: tears, in which the skin is ripped by something sharp such as a nail; clean cuts, caused by contact with a smooth, sharp cutting surface such as a piece of broken glass; punctures, caused by a thorn or nail sticking directly into the flesh but not tearing it; and bruises, which a horse or pony will collect in the same way as we do, by banging or knocking himself sharply against some object. Of these, puncture wounds are probably the most serious, unless a tear is very extensive, and this is partly because they so often go unnoticed until they begin to suppurate, which is one of the reasons why you should always run your hands down a pony's legs after exercise or when giving him his daily check for injuries. If he flinches as you touch a spot, you may be able to detect a small wound which otherwise might easily be missed.

Washing a wound

The first thing to do when you discover such an injury is to clean it so that you can assess its severity. The best way to wash a wound is to direct a gentle stream of water from a hosepipe on to it. If you have to wash the wound directly, dab round it with a large pad of very wet cotton wool as gently as possible. Do not use a sponge. These tend to be rough in texture and may also be harbouring germs. Also, do not use strong disinfectants. They will do more harm than good.

If the wound is not severe, dust it liberally with an antibiotic powder once it has been cleaned. These are usually packaged in a plastic 'puffer' bottle, which enables you to direct the powder straight on to the wound without having to handle it in any way. Thereafter, keep an eye on the wound to make sure it is healing, which it should do quite naturally on its own.

LEFT and RIGHT: In this series of pictures a nasty cut on the pastern is being treated. After the wound has been cleaned, anti-biotic powder is first applied, followed by a sterilized dressing. A thick wedge of cotton wool is wrapped right round the leg to protect the wound throughout. Finally, a crepe bandage is wound round the cotton wool for added protection.

If you feel that the wound requires professional attention – maybe a stitch – do not attempt any further treatment yourself once the wound has been cleaned. Call the veterinary surgeon and keep the pony as still and quiet as possible until he arrives.

Most cuts and bruises will occur on a pony's legs since these are the most vulnerable areas. This often makes it possible to bandage a cut if you think it needs protection. Cover the wound with a lint or a gauze-covered dressing and bandage it as lightly as possible – the aim is just to keep the bandage in place. However, in most cases it is better not to bandage a wound. Fresh air is one of the most effective cures.

If your pony does cut himself it is important to bear in mind that any infection in the wound can lead to a serious, indeed generally fatal, disease called tetanus, or 'lockjaw'. He can be immunized against this condition by a course of injections, and this is the wisest thing to do. If the pony does not have this protection, he should be given a shot of anti-tetanus serum as soon as possible after he has cut himself. In fact, even if he has had a course of injections he should still be given a booster dose if he cuts himself very badly.

Bad management

Other possible injuries you may encounter are saddle or harness sores, 'girth galls' and mouth injuries. All these are really to be deplored since they generally indicate bad management on your part. Saddle or harness sores are the result of ill-fitting or dirty tack which is so hard that it rubs sore patches on the pony's skin. These can occur anywhere where the saddle or bridle comes into contact with the animal. Girth galls are sore patches caused by the rubbing of the girth and they usually appear just behind the elbow (see page 94). The treatment for all these injuries is to stop work, since the condition will obviously be worsened if tack continues to be used. If the 'rub' of a harness sore has turned into an open wound, with the skin broken and bleeding, treat it as you would treat a cut. First clean it and then apply antibiotic powder to dry it. When the sore has healed you can harden the skin by applying salt and water or methyl-

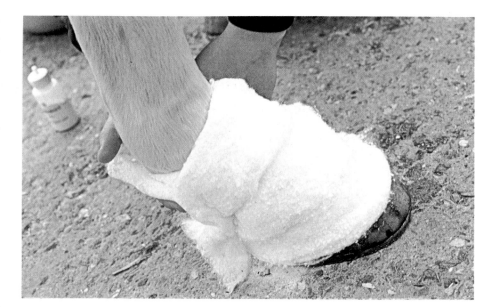

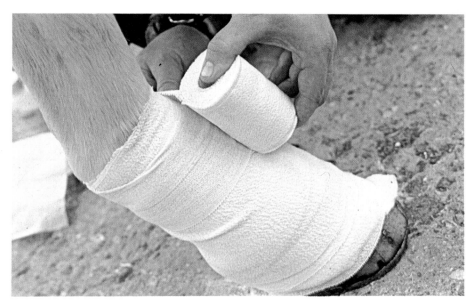

ated spirit. Using a string of nylon girth rather than a leather one will help to lessen the risk of girth galls if a pony is tender-skinned and prone to them, but if the galls persist put a pad of sheepskin or lamb's wool under the girth.

Mouth injuries result from an ill-fitting bit, rough treatment from a rider, or from using a dirty bit on which deposits of saliva have been allowed to remain so that they become hardened and rough. Bathe the sore areas with salt and water and again do not ride until they have healed. It may also be a good idea to change the bit, particularly if the injury was caused because it was ill-fitting.

Horses and ponies are subject to various skin diseases and skin con-

ditions. Among the most common of these are ringworm, 'sweet itch' and infestations of lice – the last occurring mostly in grass-kept ponies in late winter to early spring. Ringworm shows up as little circular bald patches appearing in the coat. Sweet itch affects the crest of the neck and the top of the tail, causing such intense irritation to these areas that a pony will rub them raw given the opportunity. Lice also attack these same areas with the same result. Antidote powders and ointments are available for all these ailments, so if you notice any unusual skin condition occurring anywhere on your pony, ask the veterinary surgeon to diagnose it and to prescribe accordingly.

Lameness, as we have already said, is

one of the most common causes of your pony being unfit for riding. 'Seats' of lameness can occur anywhere from the shoulders or upper thighs right down the legs to the feet, with the feet probably being the most common and the worst offenders.

Lameness

The first thing to do when your pony goes lame is to discover which leg is giving the pain. Unless he is very obviously lame in one leg, this is no easy task. If the animal is resting a foreleg, then it is almost certainly that foreleg which is the problem. Frequently the cause is less obvious and you will need to walk or trot him along a piece of even ground to find out where the trouble lies. For this you will need an assistant either to lead him or to observe while you do so. As the animal trots (and take him slowly – there is no need to add to his agony), if the problem is in a foreleg, he will bob his head down sharply when the good leg hits the ground. This allows him to raise his head as the painful leg goes down, thus putting the minimum amount of weight on it. If he is lame in a hind leg, there will again be a noticeable drop of his hindquarters (best seen by standing directly behind him) as the sound leg comes into contact with the ground.

Having determined which is the offending leg, all you need to do is to discover what is actually causing the lameness. Unless there is an obvious cut or wound present, run your hand gently down the leg, looking for any indication of heat or swelling. Also, of course, you are likely to encounter some reaction from the animal when you touch the painful spot, so be prepared for him to lift his leg sharply or to start in pain.

In just about all cases of lameness you will need to consult the veterinary surgeon for advice on treatment, if not

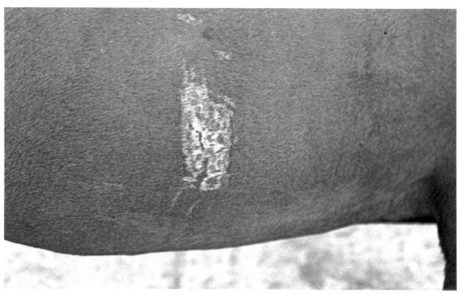

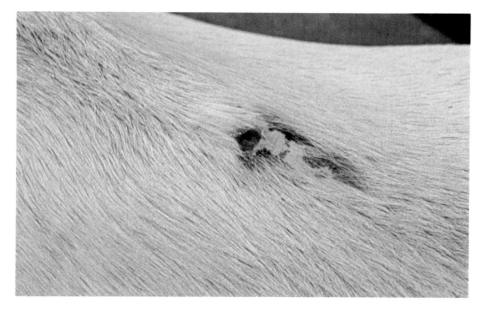

TOP: A tincture of iodine being applied to ringworm. CENTRE: A surcingle gall. BOTTOM: Saddle sores are often caused by badly fitting saddlery. Great care should always be taken to ensure that the saddle fits snugly on a horse or pony. If it does not, damage to the horse or pony will result.

for diagnosis. Some of the most commonly encountered causes for lameness are outlined below.

If the horse or pony has been asked to work hard either on very soft or very hard ground when he is not really fit, strains and sprains to various parts of the legs are likely to occur and cause lameness. Sprained tendons or ligaments of the foreleg occur just below the knee on the inside and the affected area will usually be hot and swollen. The fetlock, too, may be affected, often from a definite twist, when the whole joint is also likely to be hot and swollen. The knee joint can be similarly sprained, usually as the result of a bad fall, in which case the pony may have also sustained cuts to his knees. This condition is known as 'broken knees'. The cuts are slow to heal because of the constant movement in the joint. Usually the hair grows white over broken knees, which is a good indication of whether a horse or pony has suffered from this in the past. Sprains and strains are best treated by regular hosing with cold water for ten to fifteen minutes at a time. If the sprain is a bad one, your veterinary surgeon may recommend more drastic treatment.

Resting and hosing

Windgalls, which are puffy swellings occurring just above the fetlock on any leg, are also the result of pounding on hard ground. They often cause lameness when they first occur, but a short rest accompanied by hosing with cold water soon cures them. Avoid working the animal on hard ground again or they will soon return.

Another condition resulting from concussion to the leg is the formation of splints. These are small bony growths that occur on the splint bone or the cannon bone just behind or below the knee (see page 94). Once they have formed they usually remain for all time,

A device (top right) on the pony's head holds the jaws open while the vet feels for sharp teeth.
CENTRE: This bit injury has been caused by a badly fitting bit or by rough handling by the rider.
RIGHT: After this pony's cut mouth has been dressed he will wear a special muzzle.

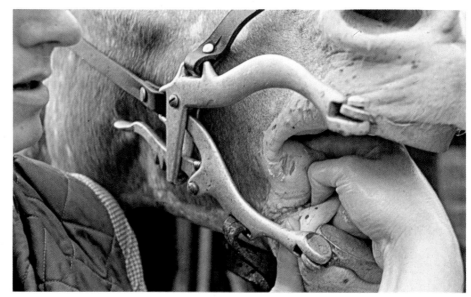

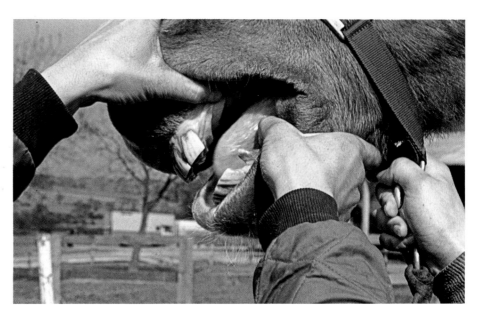

LEFT: Run your hands down the pony's leg each day to feel for any lumps or swellings. ABOVE: Walk or trot a lame pony along the road to determine which leg is causing the trouble.

but they generally only cause lameness in their early stages of growth.

Ringbones and sidebones are bony enlargements that occur on the pasterns (see page 94) or around the heel respectively. They are often caused by concussion or heavy work, particularly if this is inflicted on a young animal, but in some cases they appear to be linked to an hereditary or congenital condition. The ringbone may occur where it affects the movement in the pastern joint, while sidebones tend to interfere with the flexibility of the heel. Even with prolonged rest and expert treatment, horses and ponies rarely recover one hundred per cent from these afflictions and tend to show some lameness on hard ground thereafter.

Sprains to the tendons or ligaments in the hind leg result in curbs. The area just below the back of the hock becomes swollen, hot and tender. Curbs can usually be cured quite easily but you should stop work immediately and seek professional advice. If they are allowed to go untreated they can result in recurrent lameness. Bog and bone spavins also affect the area around the hock, although both occur on the inside rather than directly on the outside like a curb. A bog spavin is a soft swelling on the front of the hock joint which does not always cause lameness. A bone spavin, on the other hand, usually does lead to lameness. This is a bony growth on the inside of the leg just below the hock. Both may be caused by strain or by some slight congenital defect. Rest, hosing and massage are generally the prescribed treatment. A thoroughpin is

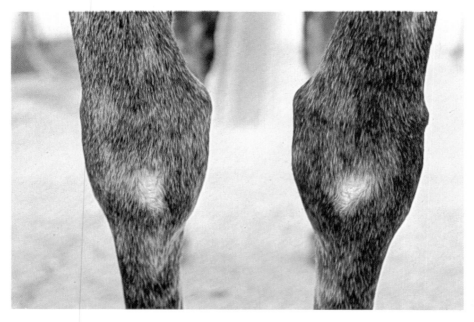

ABOVE: Broken knees are the tell-tale evidence that the pony has at some time had a bad fall. The hair always grows white over such injuries sustained to the knees.
LEFT: An horrendous example of the damage and injury that can be caused by barbed wire. Avoid letting your pony come into contact with barbed wire at all times and on no account use barbed wire for fencing off your field.
RIGHT: Letting a pony stand for fifteen to twenty minutes in a stream is extremely soothing for his tired legs – especially if he has carried you a long way. He will much appreciate the break.

a soft swelling that affects the side of the hock joint and can usually be pushed through from one side of the leg to the other. This is similar to a windgall and is likewise caused by concussion and strain. It can be relieved by gentle massage, accompanied by rest.

Two possible causes of self-inflicted lameness are brushing and overreaching. Brushing is when a horse hits the area around the fetlock on the fore or hind leg with the opposite fore or hind leg. Overreaching is when the toe of one or both hind legs strikes and, as often happens, cuts the heel of the forelegs. In both cases, the resulting injury should be treated accordingly. Any recurrence can be prevented by equipping the horse or pony with brushing or over-reach boots to protect the vulnerable areas. Shoeing with special types of shoe can also be of considerable help in preventing injury in either case.

The commonest cause

In spite of the previous discussion on causes of lameness, it is the feet, as stated earlier, that are the commonest cause. The problem, which is often related to some aspect of shoeing, will be discussed later. In addition, however, there are some diseases of the feet that can cause lameness. But before considering these it may be as well to look briefly at the construction of the foot so that you will be able to recognize and understand some of the problem areas that you may have to deal with.

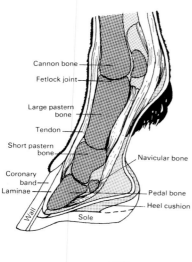

Cannon bone
Fetlock joint
Large pastern bone
Tendon
Short pastern bone
Coronary band
Laminae
Wall
Navicular bone
Pedal bone
Heel cushion
Sole

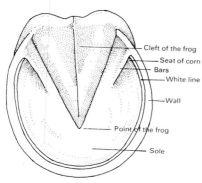

Cleft of the frog
Seat of corn
Bars
White line
Wall
Point of the frog
Sole

The outer covering of the foot – the part we see – is called the 'wall' and is tough, horny and insensitive. Its insensitivity means that nails can be driven into it to hold the shoe in place without the animal feeling any pain. This outer covering grows in the same way as a fingernail, from the top, or the coronet, downwards and, like fingernails, it must be kept trimmed to prevent it from growing too long. Immediately behind the wall of the hoof is a sensitive area known as the *laminae*. This can become infected if, for example, a nail is inadvertently hammered into it instead of into the wall. Infection of the laminae is intensely painful for a horse or pony since, because it is encased by the horn, there is no room for the area to swell and expand.

The under-surface of the foot consists of a flat area of soft, horny material called the 'sole' and a v-shaped area of

These diagrams show two views of the foot – from the side and from underneath the hoof.

leather horn called the 'frog'. The sole is comparatively tough and as such protects the underside of the foot, but it can quite easily be bruised or pierced by anything sharp. The frog is the first part of the foot to come into contact with the ground and so takes the impact of the step, thus lessening any possible jar to the legs. It therefore acts as an anti-concussion device and as a general shock-absorber. Its leathery composition and its wedge shape also give it properties of grip, so that it acts, too, as an anti-slip pad. As we can see, the frog is of paramount importance to a pony and it is therefore essential to keep it clean and healthy. The sides of the frog and the cleft in the middle should always be carefully and meticulously kept free from dirt. This can be done when the pony's feet are being picked out with the hoof pick.

The two most serious diseases of the foot are probably *laminitis* and *navicular*, both of which seem to affect ponies more frequently than they do horses. Laminitis is an inflammation of the laminae behind the wall of the hoof. It

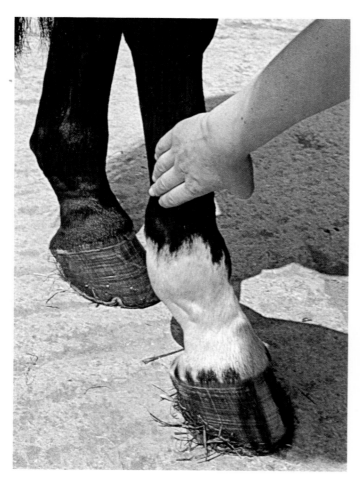

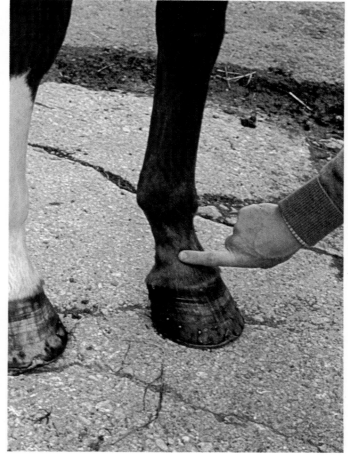

can affect both the hind and the forefeet or, more generally, just the forefeet. It is an acutely painful disease as can be seen by a pony's reluctance to put any weight on his feet when he is so afflicted. It may be caused by strenuous work on hard ground when the pony is unfit, or by allowing him to overindulge on rich spring grass or heating foods such as oats or pulses. The shoes should be removed at once and the food intake drastically reduced. Keeping the feet wet, either with poultices or constant hosing, or tethering the pony up so that he stands in a stream of running water will help to relieve the condition. Your veterinary surgeon will recommend any further treatment and will probably also give pain-relieving injections as required.

Navicular is, if anything, more serious since there appears to be no permanent cure. This is a condition resulting from the formation of an ulcer on the navicular bone, which is one of the small bones that make up the foot. It can result from serious concussion but is more usually the result of a congenital conformation defect whereby the pony has short, upright pasterns rather than long sloping ones. Symptoms of navicular are a pointing of one or either forefoot in turn and a general shortening in stride, accompanied by a tendency to put weight on the toes rather than on the heels. Once a veterinary surgeon has diagnosed navicular, the most usual course of action is to have the animal destroyed. A relieving of the condition, rather than a cure, can sometimes be brought about but the animal will never be fit for more than the very lightest of work.

Less serious

Another fairly common disease of the foot, and one that is far less serious, is thrush. This occurs when the frog becomes infected, often because the horse or pony has been left to stand on wet, dirty bedding for prolonged periods. Thrush is a most unpleasant disease, in that the frog exudes a foul-smelling discharge. Treatment is by cleaning the frog regularly and dressing it with a dry powder. Consult your vet as to which preparation is the best to use. Thereafter, of course, make sure that the bedding is always kept clean, dry and hygienic.

The horn of the hoof on some horses and ponies is particularly brittle and subject to cracking. If cracks begin at the bottom of the foot, they are not generally very serious and will usually be dealt with on re-shoeing. Those that begin at the top of the foot are called 'sand cracks' and need more careful attention, particularly as they tend to open up as they extend down the foot and so may become infected. A black-

The pictures at the bottom of these pages show, left to right: windgalls, puffy swellings around the top of the fetlock joint, caused by concussion; ringbone, a chronic condition in which a bony lump forms just beneath the fetlock; laminitis – the horizontal rings running round the hoof are evidence; cracked heels, caused by long periods spent in very wet or muddy conditions.

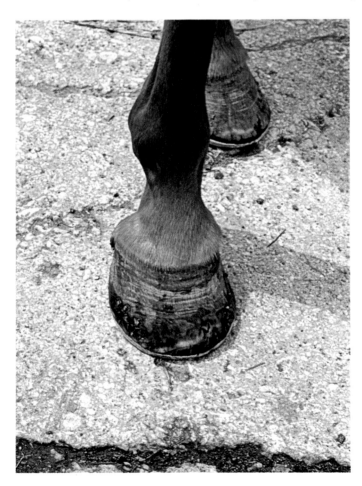

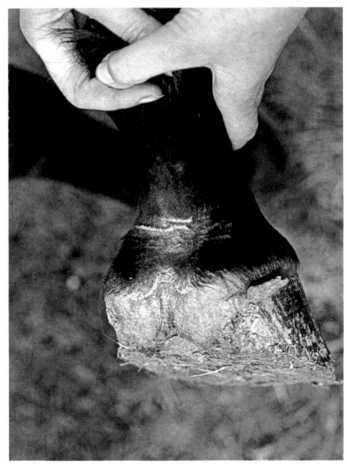

maintaining the feet in good condition. Shoeing is done by the farrier, who is a trained and skilled craftsman. He makes the shoes, fits them to the animal's feet and hammers them in place by driving nails into the wall of the foot from the underneath so that they emerge on the outside of the hoof. The ends of the nails are then clipped off and the small piece left protruding is hammered against the wall and filed to make it smooth. These tiny nail ends are called 'clenches'.

Hot and cold shoeing

There are two ways of shoeing – hot and cold – and the terms are self-explanatory. Preparation of the foot is the same in each case. The farrier first removes the old shoe, then he pares the excess horn with an instrument called a 'drawing knife' and files the edge of the foot with a rasp to make it flat and smooth. Finally, he fits the shoe to the foot. In the case of hot shoeing, he chooses a shoe that as near as possible fits the foot, and heats the shoe in the fire. While it is still hot he presses it on to the sole of the foot and burns off the excess horn (this causes the animal no pain). The farrier is then able to see if any further adjustments are needed to make the shoe fit more exactly and these he will do while the metal of the shoe is still soft. He cools the shoe by immersing it in water before nailing it in place on the foot.

In cold shoeing, all adjustments to the shoe are made by hammering at the hard metal, without the benefit of making it more malleable by heating. Also, the excess horn is not burned off, thus making the cutting down of the foot a more exacting task for the farrier. These two points combine to mean that such an exact fit is seldom achieved. However, cold shoeing is perfectly satisfactory and the advent of more and more 'travelling farriers' means that it is the most generally practised system.

The frequency with which horses and ponies will need shoeing will depend to a large extent on how much and how hard they are being worked. As a general rule, however, most horses

ABOVE: The farrier hammers at a shoe on the anvil, slightly altering it to fit the pony's foot. LEFT: The groove of the shoe and the nail heads are clearly visible on the newly-shod foot.

smith or farrier will assist in treating the condition. In bad cases the crack will have to be cleaned out and possibly some clips or clasps inserted into the wall of the hoof to try to bring the sides together.

The fitting and securing of iron shoes to the feet of horses and ponies kept for riding or work purposes is essential to

ABOVE RIGHT: The Farrier hammers the shoe into place. RIGHT: Cold shoeing in an emergency.

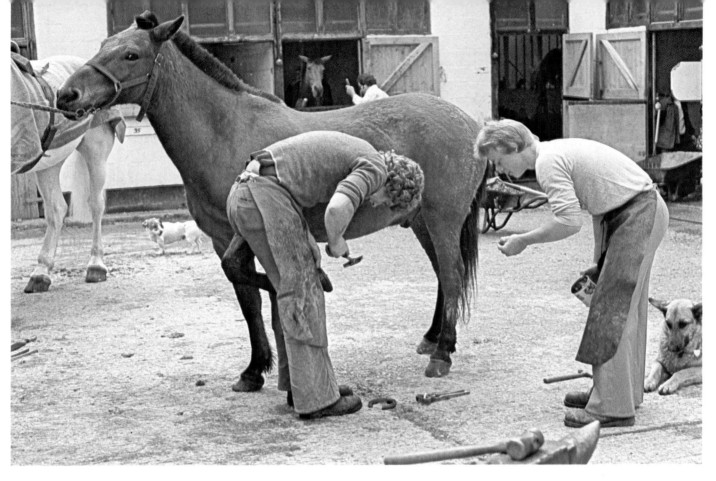

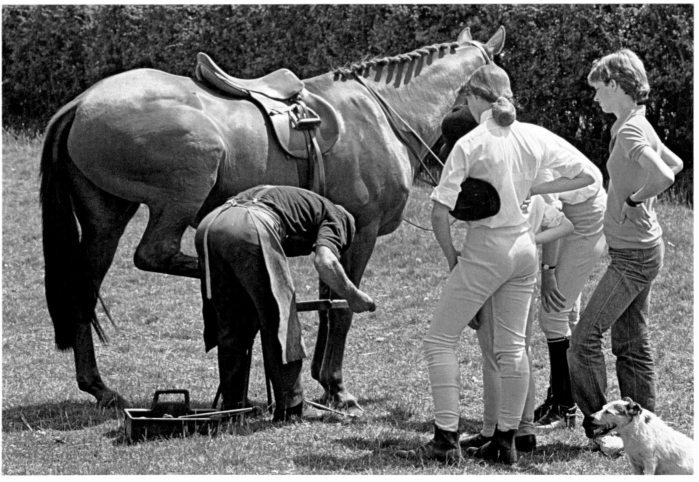

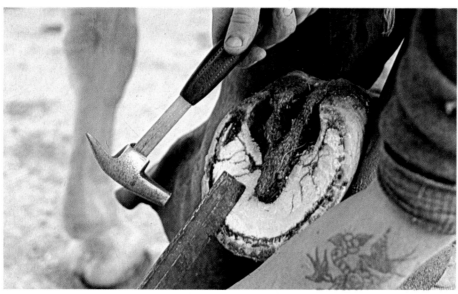

and ponies need some attention to their feet once a month. If they are being ridden regularly they will probably need new shoes at this time, but if the shoes are not really worn down the farrier may just remove them, cut back and file the feet and then replace the shoes for a little longer.

Loose shoes

Of course, the feet may need attention or the shoes may need replacing in less than a month. Watch out for the signs that will tell you a visit from the farrier is due. The shoes may become loose, when you will hear the clicking noise they make as the foot comes into contact with the ground. Alternatively the shoe may come off altogether, which is known as being 'cast', and you should stop riding until it has been replaced. If it comes off in the middle of a ride, lead – rather than ride – your pony home. Often a pony will wear down one side of the shoe at a faster rate than the other, when replacement will be necessary, or the clenches may begin to rise, that is, the nail ends will stick up and stand away from the wall of the hoof. In this state they can cause minor injuries if the pony strikes another leg with the offending foot. The final indication is if the foot has grown very long so that it is extending over the side of the shoes.

A newly shod foot should look neat and even. The horn should have been pared equally and evenly all round to maintain the symmetrical shape of the foot. The bottom of the foot should be flat and even, so that no daylight shows between the foot and the shoes. The clenches should be evenly spaced round the hoof, all at the same distance from the ground. Above all, the shoe should not be so high or the back of the hoof so long that the frog no longer comes into contact with the ground, otherwise it cannot do its shock-absorbing job properly.

Most horses and ponies will be shod with a standard, simple shoe, generally known as a 'hunter shoe'. The surface

TOP LEFT: The farrier pulls off the old, worn, shoe. CENTRE: Paring away excess horn from the bottom of the hoof. BOTTOM LEFT: A good example of hot shoeing.

that comes into contact with the ground has a deep groove in it, which helps to give a better grip than a smooth surface would. There are, however, many different types of shoe available, whether designed to suit particular work conditions or to help in treating problems an animal may have with his feet. If, for example, a pony has a badly bruised sole, caused perhaps by stepping on a sharp flint, the farrier may recommend shoeing the foot with a leather-soled shoe. In this way the sole is completely protected. If the pony has corns, which occur at the heel by the top sides of the frog, he would probably advise shoeing with three-quarter shoes which leave the troubled areas free. Corns, incidentally, can be caused by badly-fitting shoes that pinch.

Of course, all farriers know their job and are fully aware of the problems a horse or pony can have with his feet, but occasionally lameness can be caused by a slip on their part. If your pony does go lame a day or two after seeing the farrier, check his feet, just in case the cause lies there. For example, a nail could be pressing against the sensitive laminae – a condition known as 'nail binding' – or the farrier may have inadvertently pricked the sole of the foot with a nail, and this will also soon cause lameness.

Get off and walk

A final word about lameness whatever its cause may be – never ride a lame pony under any circumstances until he is sound again. If he goes lame during a ride, unless you can determine the cause and correct it on the spot (and this will only be likely if the cause is not more than a stone lodged in one of his shoes), then you must get off and lead him home. In extreme cases, if he is very badly lame or you have a long way to go, it may be necessary to arrange

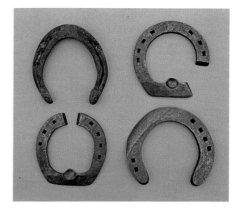

ABOVE: Some of the tools used by the farrier for the shoeing of horses and ponies. The bottom picture shows surgical shoes.

transport to get him home. Never make the condition worse by riding him and thereby adding to his burden. You might turn a less serious condition into something chronic.

113

6 All about tack

We do not know exactly when man first realized the advantages he would have if he mastered the horse by riding on its back rather than by using it as a harness, or pack, animal. We do know, however, that having once mounted it and ridden it to pursue other beasts of the plains, he did not take long to discover that some form of tack would give him greater control, and hence greater mastery, over this, the most useful of animals.

The bridle was the first such item to evolve, which is perhaps not surprising. After all, it must have become apparent at a very early stage that a device attached to the horse's head and controlled by the rider would give the rider much greater opportunity to change the animal's direction and pace as required. The horse's mouth is one of its most sensitive zones and the fact was exploited by putting some sort of 'bar' into it. The bridle in its crudest form, consisting of a bar, or 'bit', to which a pair of reins were attached and held in position in the mouth by a strap passing over the animal's head, is known to have been in use for about two thousand years. Many of the early bits were more elaborate than those in use today but they differ remarkably little from each other in principle.

Saddle origins

The saddle came considerably later than the bridle. It would seem that overcoming the discomfort of riding bareback was of less importance to early man than gaining control over the animal from a mounted position. The saddle began life as a blanket or pad thrown over the horse's back to give a rider fractionally more comfort. In all probability, however, it was the invention of the stirrup that led to more sophisticated designs of the saddle, as a vehicle for supporting the irons. The stirrup owes much of its origin to the fact that horses became more and more

The familiar picture of an immaculately groomed horse and rider at a horse show.

A Camargue pony wearing the traditional saddle used by the 'cowboys' of the Camargue.

'beasts of war' to be ridden into battle against the enemy. It did not take the early warriors long to realize two things. Firstly, that by lifting their seats clear of the horse's back and leaning forward their mounts could move faster. Secondly, and if anything more significant within the context of war, that by having some support for their feet, and thus a more secure position on the horse's back, mounted warriors were able to stand up and thrust more effectively with their swords and lances.

A further important factor that influenced the design of the saddle was that bareback riding eventually leads to serious injury to the horse's spine since the rider's weight is concentrated directly on this vulnerable area. A well-designed saddle takes the rider's weight off the spine and distributes it evenly over the fleshy muscles that protect the rib cage, where it does not harm the animal. These considerations would have greatly affected the design of the saddle and they account for the elaborate framework upon which saddles are constructed today.

The bridle

Over the centuries, the bridle has had many additions and refinements made to it, but its basic design and the principle upon which it functions remain the same. Its main purpose is still to hold the bit in the horse's mouth in order to give the rider the maximum opportunity to control his mount. The simplest bridle of all is a snaffle (this term actually applying to the bit), although there are many different types of snaffle bit.

The bridle consists of the bit and a number of leather straps. The bit is attached on either side to a short leather cheek strap which buckles on to the headpiece, a longer piece of leather that passes over the head. The sides are further divided into the throatlash, consisting of a long strap that passes under the animal's throat to buckle at the side of his head. The headpiece is prevented from slipping backwards down the animal's neck by the brow-band, which is a short strip of leather with a loop at either end that slides on to the headpiece. The browband lies in front of the horse's ears.

The reins

Also attached to the bit are the reins. These are usually made of leather and may be of varying thickness, plaited or laced according to the rider's preference. Plaited or laced reins do not slip in wet conditions, either in heavy rain or if the horse is sweating profusely on his neck. The same principle applies to rubber-covered reins, which are most often used on racehorses. Reins may also be made of nylon or string. All reins attach to the bit either by a buckle, a stud or by being permanently stitched. A buckle or stud fastening is more satisfactory than stitching from the point of view of cleaning and the stud is neater in appearance than the buckle. These same fastening methods apply to attaching the cheekpieces to the bit – the stud type again being the neatest in appearance.

Most bridles nowadays carry a nose-band. Once more there are many different types of noseband, designed for different purposes. The simplest type of all is the cavesson, which is a strap of varying widths that encircles the nose about 5 cm (2 in) above the corners of the mouth. It is kept in place by a thin strap that passes over the top of the head, through the loops of the browband to lie beneath the headpiece, and buckles along the horse's cheek. Unless a standing martingale (see page 124) is attached to this noseband, the cavesson fulfils no actual function and is there purely for appearance. Many people think it enhances the look of the animal's face, Other nosebands have been designed for specific purposes and these will be discussed in greater detail later.

One of the most common of the

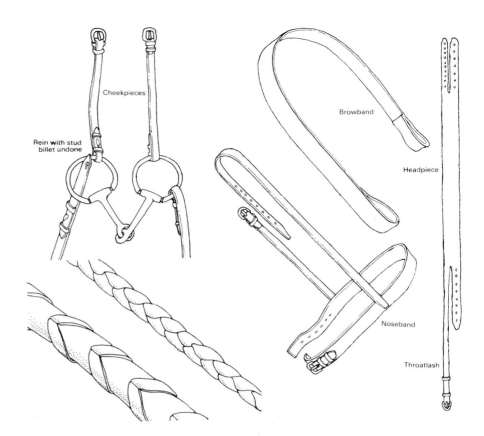

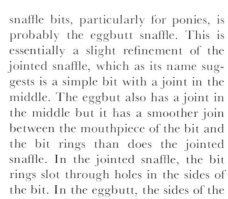

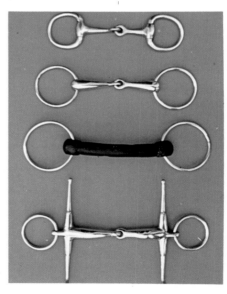

snaffle bits, particularly for ponies, is probably the eggbutt snaffle. This is essentially a slight refinement of the jointed snaffle, which as its name suggests is a simple bit with a joint in the middle. The eggbut also has a joint in the middle but it has a smoother join between the mouthpiece of the bit and the bit rings than does the jointed snaffle. In the jointed snaffle, the bit rings slot through holes in the sides of the bit. In the eggbutt, the sides of the

These diagrams show the various parts of the bridle and, inset, laced and plaited reins.
ABOVE LEFT: The top two bits make up the double bridle – the bridoon (small snaffle) and Weymouth curb. Beneath is a Kimblewick. ABOVE RIGHT: Examples of the snaffle bit. From the top: the eggbutt, a plain jointed, a rubber snaffle and a snaffle with cheeks.

bit in effect form part of the rings, so the rings are not movable. Provided the mouthpiece is fairly thick, the jointed and eggbutt snaffles are both mild bits. In the hands of a sympathetic rider, pressure is exerted on the corners of the mouth (which are less sensitive than the 'bars', that is, the non-fleshy area between the front and back teeth) and on the tongue in a nutcracker action caused by the joint in the middle.

The mildest of all bits is the half-moon, or straight-bar, unjointed snaffle, which may be made of metal, rubber or vulcanite. Again, the thicker it is the milder it is since the edges are correspondingly more rounded and smooth. Other snaffle bits are the twisted snaffle and gag snaffle, both of which are very severe and should only ever be used by experts. The twisted snaffle has a mass of sharp edges caused by the twists, and the gag is so rigged that pressure is also brought to bear on the poll (see page 94). The Fulmer snaffle is more frequently seen, particularly in use with a dropped noseband (see page 126). It has a jointed mouthpiece and long, straight cheekpieces extending perpendicularly from the mouthpiece inside the bit rings. These are held firm by small leather loops attached to the bridle's cheekpieces, so keeping the mouthpiece of the bit more static in the animal's mouth.

Curb bits

Many pony owners favour one of the Pelham or curb bits and it does seem that they often suit small, somewhat headstrong animals. The Pelham is essentially a combination of the bits in a double bridle, which we will look at first. The double bridle consists of two bits, a bridoon, which is similar to an ordinary jointed snaffle except it has a thinner mouthpiece and smaller bit rings, and a curb bit, known as a 'Weymouth'. This has a pair of rings for the reins situated at the bottom of the downward cheekpiece. The mouthpiece has a slight 'port', which is a

A double bridle (above right) has two bits – a bridoon and a Weymouth curb. This gives precision control. RIGHT: An ordinary snaffle bridle. This simple bridle is ideal for most ponies.

feature of many curb bits. 'Port' is the name given to the centre of the mouthpiece when it is raised to any degree. This gives more tongue room but it also assists in causing the bit to exert pressure on the bars of the mouth. In extreme cases, if the port is very high it can press against the roof of the mouth when the reins are used. The Weymouth bit has a curb chain attached to it, which lies outside the mouth in the chin groove and again, as the reins are used, presses against this area. The two bits of a double bridle each have their own set of reins and a separate headpiece to hold them in place. The principle of the double bridle is that the bridoon acts on the corners of the mouth, which has the effect of raising the animal's head carriage, while the Weymouth acts on the bars of the mouth and the chin groove, causing the animal to flex his neck and jaw. Thus a rider using a double bridle has a greater degree of control over both the animal's head carriage and his movements. For this reason, the double bridle is most frequently seen in use in the show and dressage rings where such refinement of control is needed. The bits are not over-severe but, as might be imagined, the double bridle should only be used by those riders who understand its operation and are competent to use it correctly.

Pelham bits

The Pelham, mentioned earlier, combines in just one bit the action of the two bits in a double bridle, although the rider still has to handle and manipulate two pairs of reins. As with the snaffle there are a number of different types of Pelham bit. All have straight (as opposed to jointed) mouthpieces and they may or may not have a port. In addition, they all have facilities for attaching a curb chain and they should always be used in conjunction with one. There are two pairs of rings for the reins on Pelham bits, a larger pair immediately to the side of the

ABOVE LEFT: An ordinary Pelham bridle which has one bit to which two reins are attached. A curb chain lies under the chin.
LEFT: This severe bridle is known as a gag.

mouthpiece and a smaller pair situated at the bottom of the cheekpiece – generally about 4–5 cm (1½–2 in) lower than the top pair. The long cheekpiece operates like a lever. When the rider exerts pressure on the bottom reins, the curb chain is brought into the chin groove by the action of the lever. The links of the curb chain should always be turned so that they lie flat in the groove. The chain should never be fastened too tightly. If the curb chain does rub at the skin in the groove for any reason, rubber or sheepskin guards can be fitted over it. The curb chain may be further held in place by a thin leather lip strap, which buckles on to the tiny rings situated between the two pairs of bit rings. The strap passes through the extra link in the centre of the curb chain, so it is essential that this link should always be at the bottom of the chain when it is twisted flat.

Kimblewick bit

If a rider finds two pairs of reins too much of a handful and yet wants to use a Pelham bit on his pony, it is possible to use just one pair of reins by attaching these not to the bit rings but to a small leather loop, or coupling, that can be used to link the bit rings. However, in doing so you somewhat lose the benefit of the independent function of each pair of reins. A further alternative would be to use a Kimblewick bit, which has become increasingly popular since its invention some thirty years ago. The Kimblewick has a straight mouthpiece with a slight port in the centre and large D-shaped rings for the rein (a single pair only). It also possesses hooks for a curb chain. It is therefore similar to the other Pelham bit but is, in fact, rather milder although it gives greater control than the simple snaffle bits.

Guidelines on how tightly the throatlash and noseband should be buckled were given in Chapter one. The other important aspect of fitting a bridle correctly concerns, of course, the bit. It should rest gently against the corners of the animal's mouth without either wrinkling them, which indicates it is too high in the mouth, or banging against the lower teeth, in which case it is obviously too low.

In addition to the bits and bridles discussed, some people choose to ride

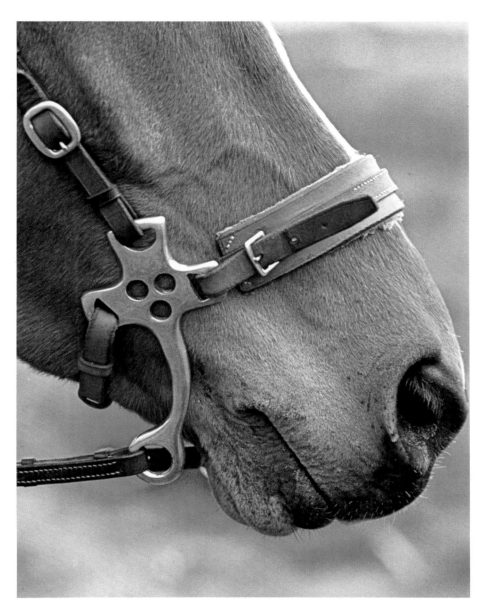

A bitless bridle known as the Hackamore. It applies pressure to the top of the head and nose.

their horses in bitless bridles. The name is self-explanatory. The most common type of bitless bridle is the Hackamore, of which there are various designs.

Many horses go better in a bitless bridle, particularly if they have experienced rough treatment from a heavy-handed rider when wearing a bit or if they have sore, bruised or excessively sensitive mouths. However, the Hackamore is not always the mild contraption many people believe it to be and great discretion should be exercized when using it.

The principle of a Hackamore is to exert pressure on the nose and the curb groove, both of which are sensitive areas. The noseband and strap that passes under the chin are attached to metal cheekpieces, which vary in length according to the design. The reins are attached to rings at the end of the cheekpieces and, when operated by the rider, cause pressure to be exerted on the nose and chin groove. The longer the metal cheekpieces, the greater the leverage and therefore the greater the force applied through the reins.

The Hackamore can be made more severe by using a narrow, rather than a wide, strap across the nose. A narrow, rough-textured strap will obviously exert more direct pressure than a wider one. The mildest of all is a wide leather strap covered in sheepskin.

The strap that goes under the chin

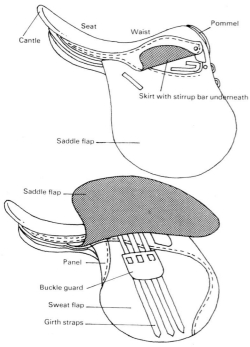

The parts of a saddle:
- Cantle
- Seat
- Waist
- Pommel
- Skirt with stirrup bar underneath
- Saddle flap

- Saddle flap
- Panel
- Buckle guard
- Sweat flap
- Girth straps

should be made of leather. A chain, as used with a curb bit, is too severe in most cases since the pressure exerted on the chin groove when using a bitless bridle is considerably greater than is the case with a bit.

Saddle design

As mentioned earlier, the saddle developed later than the bridle, probably as man became aware of the greater comfort it would give him and his horse and the additional security and control afforded as he sat on the animal's back.

Over the years a number of different saddles have evolved to suit the requirements of different aspects of horsemanship. Stockmen and cowboys, who have to spend many hours a day in the saddle during the course of their regular work,

The parts of a saddle showing the components and the underneath when the flap is lifted.

The Western or stock saddle is designed to make a long day in the saddle as easy as possible.

use quite a different saddle from the sort you would use when you go out for a hack. The cowboy's saddle, known as a western, or stock, saddle, has a considerably higher back than saddles styled for English or European riding. Also, the pommel (see diagram) is greatly extended to form the tall saddle horn. This became part of the design of the stock saddle to provide an anchorage to which the end of a rope can be secured when the cowboy has roped a cow or bull. In addition, there are a number of other refinements which help the cowboy in his work and provide greater comfort and protection for his long hours in the saddle.

The saddle most frequently used in ordinary leisure riding is either the hunting saddle or the general-purpose saddle. The hunting saddle is, in fact, the older more traditional design of saddle and has been in use for many generations. More recently it has been largely superseded by the various types of general-purpose saddle. These are a little more comfortable than the hunting saddle, often having a deeper seat and 'knee rolls' at the front of the flaps. This design developed as a result of the 'forward seat', which is the standard method of riding adopted nowadays. In previous times, a rider would lean back in the saddle, sitting on the fleshy part of his buttocks, his legs pushed forward and his feet right 'home' in the stirrup irons, that is, the weight being taken on the instep rather than on the balls of the feet. At the beginning of this century, the Italians began to favour a style of riding in which the rider sat in the middle of his saddle with his weight on his seat bones and his upper body held upright or sometimes inclined slightly forward, but never backward. His legs hung straight down rather than being pushed forward and the balls of his feet rested in the irons. Although this new style was discredited at first, its value soon became obvious when it was seen how much better the horse responded. It became known as the 'forward seat' and the design of the saddle changed accordingly to accommodate it. Initially the saddle was known as a 'forward cut saddle' and was mostly used for jumping. Later the design was modified and copied the world over until it became known as the 'general-purpose saddle'.

There are, of course, other types of saddle that you will see on different occasions. The racing saddle, for example, is very light so the hose carries the minimum of static weight. The show saddle is cut with straight saddle flaps so as to show off the animal's shoulder, while the polo saddle has a cut-away section at the pommel to

The all-purpose saddle is the one most commonly used for leisure riding (top right). The side saddle is balanced by an extra strap on the right-hand side attached to the back of the saddle. This prevents the saddle slipping to the left which is the side that holds the rider's weight.

allow for maximum freedom of movement in twisting and turning at high speed. The dressage saddle is less padded and thinner than other saddles, enabling the rider to come into closer contact with his mount.

Most saddles, apart from the stock saddle, comprise the same component parts, which you should know by name (see diagram page 120). Also, they are generally constructed in a similar fashion, beginning with an inner framework known as a 'tree'. At one time this was always made of wood, but now a lightweight metal is more frequently used. It is the tree that forms the arch over the pony's spine so that this area will have no weight brought to bear upon it. The tree is covered with strips of linen and webbing, to which the wadding that will form the shape of the saddle is attached. The wadding has to be built up on the seat and underneath the tree to form the thick panels that will rest and distribute the weight evenly on the pony's back, on either side of the spine. The saddle will eventually be covered with leather and the various saddle flaps and girth straps will be attached. The underneath of the saddle may be lined with leather, linen or serge. Leather is the most expensive but is probably also the most popular. It is the easiest to keep clean but it must be kept soft and supple. A dirty saddle lining may easily cause saddle sores.

Saddle fit

The fit of the saddle is, of course, of paramount importance. First of all, there should be no pressure on the pony's spine. In fact, you should be able to see daylight through the central arch, or gullet, of the saddle from the withers or from the back to the front, even when someone is sitting in the saddle. The top of the pommel should come about 4–5 cm ($1\frac{1}{2}$–2 in) above the withers so that it does not press upon this sensitive area. Another way of assessing this is to ensure that you can get two fingers' breadth between the withers and the top of the saddle arch when you are seated in the saddle. The front arch of the saddle is often too narrow for the pony's back, so that it pushes the pommel too high above the withers. This leads to pinching. The weight of the saddle and rider should

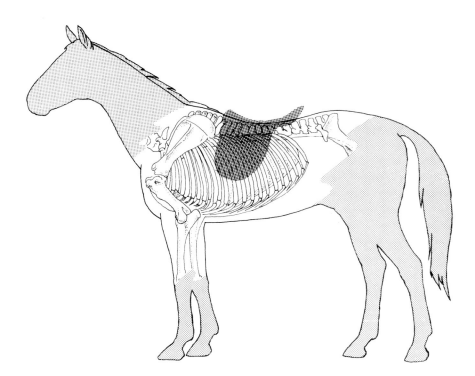

The correct position of the saddle on a horse in relation to his anatomy is shown here.

both be evenly distributed over the pony's sides, and the movement of the animal's shoulders should not in any way be impeded by the saddle. Both of these factors depend on the correct stuffing of the panels of the underneath of the saddle and it should be remembered that these become flattened and uneven after prolonged, regular use. In fact, a new saddle will need restuffing fairly soon, for the stuffing compresses very rapidly in a new saddle. If you notice that the saddle is beginning to bear down on the withers or spine or appears to be affecting the shoulder movement in any way, you should have a saddler inspect the saddle for you. Putting a blanket or pad beneath the saddle to relieve such pressure should only ever be a temporary measure, for it is simply not effective in the long term. The pony will still feel the pressure from the badly fitting saddle through the blanket.

The saddle is held in place on the pony's back by the girth, which passes under the animal's tummy and buckles to the girth straps on either side of the saddle, under the large, outside flap. The girths may be made of a variety of materials, most commonly leather,

nylon, string or webbing. At one time, leather girths were probably the most common and they are still available in various designs. If leather is used, it must be kept clean, soft and supple or it will very quickly cause girth galls. Leather girths are otherwise strong and very satisfactory. However, they are probably less often seen nowadays than nylon girths, which are an innovation of the last couple of decades. Nylon girths are similar in design to string ones – that is, several long, thin strands joined together at intervals and with a pair of buckles at either end – but they are easier to keep clean. String and nylon girths are both less likely to cause girth galls than leather on account of their texture and design. Webbing girths are seldom used nowadays, although there are some efficient new designs in this material. The old webbing girths were found not to wear well, nor to be very safe as they were subject to wearing through unexpectedly.

Stirrup leathers

Stirrup leathers and irons form the other part of the saddle. The stirrup leathers are long strips of leather held in place by the metal stirrup bars that lie at the top of the saddle flaps on either side of the saddle just below the seat. The bars usually have a small, jointed fastening at the end, which can be pushed upright once the leather has been slid into place, to ensure that it is held securely. It is essential that the stirrup leathers are kept in good condition and checked regularly to make sure that the stitching is secure and that the holes where they are usually buckled are not showing signs of wear. Have them shortened and re-stitched at the buckle end occasionally, so that new holes come into use.

Stirrup irons

Stirrup irons are made of metal, preferably steel, and are available in various designs. They provide support for the feet. The most important point about them is that they should be wide enough to ensure that your riding boot cannot get wedged in them. Conversely, they should not be so wide that your foot can slip right through. The correct-sized iron for you is about 2.5 cm (1 in) wider than your boot at its widest point.

The part of the iron where the foot rests is generally roughened to prevent the foot from slipping. After a while, however, their surface becomes smooth with wear, at which time it may be advisable to fit rubber stirrup treads. These small rubber pads just fit on to the bottom of the iron and help to prevent the foot from slipping.

It is not really necessary to examine the different types of stirrup iron, which do not differ greatly in design. However, one type of stirrup recommended by some people is the safety iron. This follows the conventional stirrup design, except that one side is not made of metal but consists of a strong rubber band. This should come on the outside of the iron when the rider's foot is placed in it – the theory being that any unusual pressure on the rubber band will release the rider's foot.

Besides the basic saddles and bridles described, other items of tack will be seen in common use on horses and

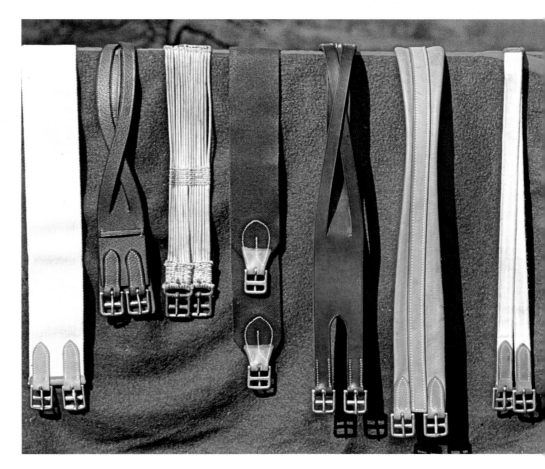

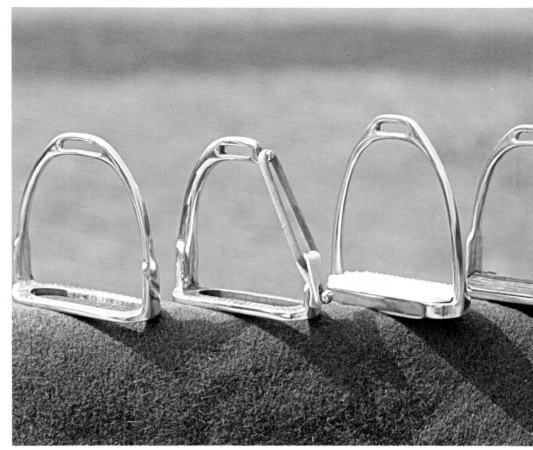

ABOVE: A Lampwick girth, a Balding leather dressage girth, a nylon string girth, a pair of union web girths, a leather Balding girth, a leather Atherstone girth and a tubular web show girth. BELOW: Stainless steel stirrup iron, German fillis iron, Peacock safety iron, traditional treadless iron.

ponies, generally either to train them or to restrain them. Perhaps the most common amongst these are martingales, which are actually classed as 'artificial aids' (see page 31).

Martingales

There are three basic types of martingale – the Irish, the standing and the running. The Irish martingale is just a short leather strap 10–15 cm (4–6 in) wide with a metal ring at either end. The reins are put through these and the martingale then lies some 15 cm (6 in) behind the horse's mouth along the reins. Its purpose is really no more than to keep the reins in place and to help prevent them going over the horse's head if the rider falls. They are quite frequently used on race horses, where it is obviously better in the event of horse and jockey parting company that the reins remain round the horse's neck rather than trail on the ground where the animal is likely to trip over them.

The standing martingale has a more restrictive purpose. It consists of a long strap attached at one end to the horse's noseband and at the other end to the girth. It is further held in place by a thin strap half-way along its length that buckles round the animal's neck. Its purpose is to prevent a horse or pony from lifting his head so high in the air that control becomes impossible. It is important, however, to remember that it should not come into effect until an animal has lifted his head high into the air. In other words, it must never be adjusted in such a way that it keeps the head down artificially. The correct fitting of a standing martingale allows you to push the strap right up into the animal's gullet when he is holding his head normally and when the strap is attached to the noseband and the girth. If it is any tighter than this, it will interfere with the natural head and neck movement and affect the animal's performance. In particular, when he is

A running martingale designed to prevent the pony from lifting his head too high.

jumping he will not be able to stretch his neck forward sufficiently to allow the necessary extension.

Running martingale

The running martingale is similar in design to the standing martingale but the strap that attaches to the noseband is instead divided into two. Each part has a metal ring at the end, which the reins are passed through. The running martingale also helps to prevent a horse or pony from raising its head too high but, because it is brought into action by

The standing martingale loops through the noseband at one end and the girth at the other.

pressure from the rider on the reins, it does not interfere with the freedom of the head in the same rigorous way as the standing martingale. Correct fitting for a running martingale allows the rings on the ends of the straps to reach to the withers when the other end is attached to the girth.

Side reins

Standing and running martingales should both be worn with a short, thick, rubber, looped 'stopper' over the join of the main strap with the neck strap. This helps to prevent the strap hanging down between the pony's forelegs, where it could be a potential danger.

Side reins are sometimes used in

training a young horse, to encourage correct head carriage. These are buckled or clipped to the bit rings and attached at the other end to the girth. The best type have a length of heavy elastic in them to allow some flexibility. Draw reins are similar and are also used to control and restrict the horse's head carriage. They are attached to the girth at one end and then pass through the bit rings and back to the rider's hand. They can be used in a very corrective manner indeed, as may be imagined, and should only be used by experts for a specific reason.

A variety of nosebands having different effects or serving different purposes will be seen in common use. The

A correctly positioned dropped noseband does not interfere with the pony's breathing.

simplest noseband, which has already been discussed, is the cavesson. It generally has no specific function other than to enhance the appearance of the horse's or pony's face. Cavessons are available in different widths and may sometimes be slightly padded and decoratively stitched when wanted for show purposes. The cavesson does have a practical use, of course, when it is used with a standing martingale.

The noseband

The dropped noseband is popular and is often seen on ponies. This is used with an ordinary jointed or eggbutt snaffle and it helps to make the bit's operation more effective by encouraging the pony to keep his mouth closed. The noseband buckles beneath the mouthpiece of the bit and its fit is therefore very important. The front part of it must come sufficiently high above the nostrils to ensure that it does not interfere with the animal's breathing, but not so high that it raises the strap at the back and causes it to pull the bit too high in the animal's mouth.

The noseband should not, of course, be buckled too tightly. As with the cavesson you should be able to get two fingers between the pony's nose and the front strap. A running martingale may be used with a dropped noseband but a standing martingale should never be used with it. The reason is obvious. It would apply pressure directly on to the low, sensitive area of the pony's nose and straightaway damage his breathing.

The Grakle noseband, also known as the cross-over, or figure-of-eight, noseband is more severe but similar in effect to the dropped noseband. It has a cross arrangement of thin leather straps, the middle of the cross coming on the animal's nose so that it exerts more direct pressure on to this area than does the dropped noseband. The bottom part of the noseband again buckles beneath the bit.

The Flash noseband combines the action of a dropped noseband at the same time as allowing a standing martingale to be worn. This noseband basically consists of a straightforward cavesson to which thinner leather straps are attached that drop down to buckle beneath the bit. The standing martingale can be attached to the

wider cavesson strap in the ordinary way.

All tack should be kept in good condition, both for reasons of safety and because doing so will help to prolong its life. Items of tack are expensive to replace. Tack that is neglected soon becomes hard, cracked and brittle. Not only does this make it uncomfortable for the horse to wear and for the rider to use, but it is liable to snap very easily at the slightest pressure and is therefore very dangerous. Clean tack will, in any event, look smarter and will show that you care about your pony and his appearance.

Cleaning tack

Ideally tack should be cleaned whenever it has been used, but if there is not time to clean it properly just wash off the bit to remove all salivary deposits, which if left will harden and become rough as they dry out. Make sure that the girth and the underneath of the saddle are clean and free from any mud or sweat marks, which could harden as they dry. Never be tempted just to soap the leather without washing it first (see page 126). Although it might produce an initial shine, soap on top of dirt produces unpleasant sticky deposits on the leather which are hard to remove. They will scratch and wear into the leather as well as producing rough spots which will soon rub into the pony's skin. This is why it is better to leave it until you have time to clean it properly.

To give your tack a thorough clean, you need a couple of buckets or bowls of warm water, clean dry sponges, saddle soap, metal polish and soft dry cloths. Put the saddle across a saddle tree, or bracket, mounted at a suitable height and remove the girths, buckle guards, stirrup leathers and stirrup irons. Slide the irons off the leathers and put them to soak in one of the buckets of water.

If there are any little black spots (these are accumulations of grease) anywhere on the leather, remove them by scratching at them very gently either with one of your nails or with a blunt knife (use the back of it to prevent any possibility of scratching the leather). Then wash all the leather thoroughly with a sponge that has been well wrung out in the warm water – not forgetting underneath the flaps and the girth straps. You should never use so much water on leather that you soak it. This will make it go hard and, in the case of the saddle, the water will probably get inside, saturate the lining and spoil it. If the underneath of the saddle is leather it, too, can be washed, but take particular care to remove all dried sweat and deposits of hair (which occurs when the animal is moulting). If it is linen, it can be lightly scrubbed. Serge is probably best treated by a thorough brushing with a dandy brush, as it takes so long to dry if it is made wet. Wash the

Cleaning the pony's tack is one of those chores which should be done at the end of a day's use.

stirrup leathers and also the girth. Again, if they are leather treat them in the same way as the rest of the leather parts. String, nylon or webbing girths should be brushed and if necessary scrubbed, using pure soap rather than a detergent, which will often irritate a horse's or pony's skin. Hang leathers and girths up to dry.

Washing the bridle

While the leather of the saddle is drying, wash the bridle. Undo all the buckles and take note of the holes where the straps should be buckled when you re-assemble the bridle. Remove the noseband and the reins and free the cheekpieces from the bit and the head-

piece. Slide the browband off the headpiece. Soak the bit together with the stirrup irons and then wash all the leather straps. Hang up each piece as you wash it or lay it out on a clean cloth or clean table. Do not put it on the ground to collect small particles of grit or dirt, which will rub into the leather when you soap it.

When all the leather has been washed and dried, soap it with saddle soap applied with a dry sponge. Rub this well in, particularly into the seat and sides of the saddle, where any excess soap could stain your riding breeches. Use a circular movement to rub the soap into these areas. If using the tinned saddle soap, there is no need

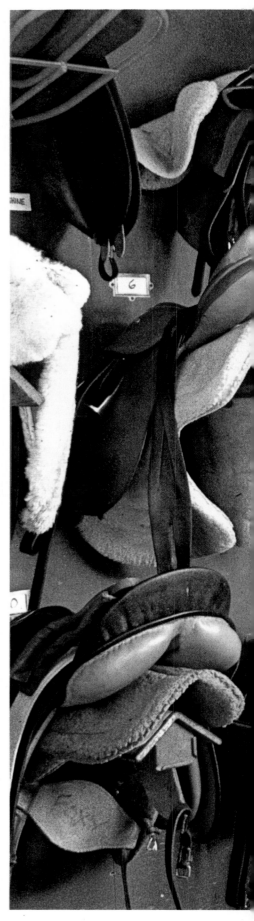

to wet it. The bar type must be dipped in water before rubbing it with the sponge but saddle soap should not produce a lather on the leather. If it does, it is too wet and will not soak into the leather properly.

Wash and dry the stirrup irons and the bit. If you like you can polish them with metal polish, but do not use metal polish on the mouthpiece of the bit – only on the bit rings.

Re-assemble the bridle and hang it up. The saddle should be replaced on its usual storage bracket. It is advisable to hang the girth, leathers and irons on suitable hooks or nails. By not re-assembling the stirrup leathers and irons and placing them back on the sides of the saddle, you will help to reduce the wear caused when the leathers are folded and the irons are resting in them.

Tack cleaning provides an excellent opportunity for checking all parts of your saddlery for signs of wear, par-

Neat rows of bridles (above) and saddles (right) hanging in a tack room after a thorough cleaning and checking. (Note the special supports to keep the saddles in good shape.)

ticularly stitching and buckle holes. If you notice any weak spots – stitches coming undone or holes getting larger – do something about them at *once*, rather than wait until they give way while you are out for a ride.

Avoid damp

Finally, make sure you keep your tack in a warm, dry place, preferably locked up to keep it safe. If the tack room is damp, this will soon affect the leather. It will absorb the dampness in the air and become sodden and somewhat slimy to the touch. It will also go darker in colour. Conversely, too hot an atmosphere will dry the leather, making it once again hard and dry, so that it will easily crack or snap.

7 Holiday in the saddle

Pony trekking and riding holidays have become increasingly popular in recent years. Many of these holiday riders have never ridden before and pony trekking, in particular, is responsible for introducing considerable numbers of people to the joys of riding.

A few essential differences between pony trekking and riding holidays have come to be generally recognized. Pony trekking holidays usually cater for beginners and novice riders as well as for more experienced horsemen and horsewomen. The main aim is to offer an opportunity for people to enjoy the beauty of the countryside on horseback, at the same time building up a relationship and understanding with the pony. On the other hand, riding holidays generally concentrate more on furthering the knowledge or ability of the rider, so the accent is usually on tuition and learning. Pony trekking holidays mean gentle rides over different distances, the longer rides taking more time, whereas riding holidays usually offer intensive instruction on a particular aspect of horsemanship or horsemastership, such as show jumping, dressage, riding side-saddle or perhaps breeding and stud management.

Riding holidays

Some riding holidays do cater for those who want to spend their holiday in the saddle riding around the local country, but these are usually run more intensively than most ordinary trekking holidays. Riders will be in the saddle all day and will then generally camp out overnight, either tethering the ponies or turning them out in a field (where previous arrangements have been made). The minimum period for such a holiday would be three days and most would go on for longer before returning to the stables. On the other hand, trekking holidaymakers rarely camp out overnight and in most instances, although different ground is covered

Pony trekkers savouring the beauty of the Austrian countryside as they gently ride downhill in the sunshine.

Riders pause for breath at the top of a rocky tor on Dartmoor – a region that is ideal for trekking.

each day, the rides start in the morning from the trekking centre. The pace of the ride is leisurely, for the ponies rarely go faster than a trot and the major part of the ride is probably conducted at a walk. This gives the riders ample opportunity to enjoy their surroundings to the full. If it is a day-long trek there is usually a stop for a picnic lunch at a predetermined place and the ride returns to the centre in the late afternoon, which means that the ride begins and ends from the same place each day.

Trekking

In this chapter we are mainly concerned with pony trekking holidays rather than with the more specialized riding holidays. In any case, all of these vary considerably. If you are thinking of going on a trekking holiday you should consider a number of points. For example, how long do you want your 'holiday in the saddle' to be and which part of the country would you like to explore in this way. Pony trekking

centres offer holidays ranging from a weekend to about a week and they may also cater for visitors who just want to ride for one day. However long you have in mind, try to find a reputable centre where you can rely on a good standard of supervision and where the ponies and equipment are properly cared for and maintained. Like the riding schools discussed in Chapter One, there are good and bad trekking centres. The bad ones are likely to push riders who may never have been on a pony's back before into the saddle on a dispirited, worn down and overworked animal and take them out for a ride without even explaining the basic rudiments of horsemanship. In addition, the tack will be in a state of neglect so that all too often it is extremely dangerous. Yet you will probably also find that the small print of your booking form states that the centre disclaims all responsibility if accidents do occur.

Admittedly it is not always possible to glean from a brochure just how well organized and reputable a centre is. To check up, contact the official national equine organization concerned with the standard of trekking centres. In the

UK, the Ponies of Britain Society has undertaken the task of inspecting trekking centres all over the country and awards certificates to those which meet its required standard.

Incidentally, they only concern themselves with conditions at the centre – that is, how the ponies are treated, the standard of instruction and supervision and the condition of tack and equipment. They do not give any guidance about the standard of accommodation and meals you can expect, so if this aspect of the holiday is of special concern to you, then make a personal investigation. Most trekking centres provide accommodation within the cost of the holiday, although this will not necessarily be at the centre itself. It could be at local guest houses or small hotel, or it may be a camping arrangement of tents or caravans. You will certainly want to know something about the accommodation offered and what meals are provided before deciding upon a particular centre.

A week's schedule

To give you an idea of what to expect on a trekking holiday, here is a day-by-day procedure for a typical week's trekking. This, in fact, runs for six days from Sunday night until Saturday night or to the following Sunday morning. Most will follow a similar pattern to the one outlined below.

Sunday night The visitors arrive at the centre, where they will be taken to their accommodation and given time to unpack and generally to settle in. Most reputable trekking centres will have given you details and some guidance on clothes suitable for trekking. Riding trousers – jodhpurs or breeches – will probably be recommended, but all will agree that strong, well-fitting jeans are quite acceptable, plus tough, buckle-free shoes or boots. If you have not already got special riding gear and this holiday is your first introduction to riding, it is probably more sensible to stick with jeans until you have made up your mind whether you want to take up riding on a more regular basis. Good trekking centres will insist that

Young trekkers are helped into the saddle, wearing hard hats provided by the trekking centre.

everyone wears a hard hat and may well provide them if you are without. Check this point when you make your booking. Take an anorak or some waterproof coat with you, too. You will be lucky to have a week with no rain.

At an appointed time, which may be before or after the evening meal, you will all gather to meet the instructors who will be taking you out for your treks. The chief instructor will probably outline the day-by-day procedure and if he or she does not already have details of your riding ability, you may also be questioned to determine your experience. Do not worry if you have no experience. You will find you are not alone. Depending on the size of the group, the instructor may attempt to split you up into smaller groups at this point or may wait until the following day when you are actually astride your ponies and your proficiency can be more accurately judged.

Although people of the same standards will probably be put together, this does not necessarily mean that the more experienced riders will go faster. It may mean that they can go over slightly more tricky country – say, where there are a lot of steep hills or streams to cross – but it does not mean they will be galloping around the countryside. That is not the purpose of trekking!

Monday After breakfast, all visitors will be expected to arrive at the centre's stables around 9.00 am. The staff, instructors and ponies will already be gathered, waiting to greet you. Most of this first morning will be taken up with fairly detailed instructions on the daily care of the trekking pony.

You will be shown how to put on a headcollar and tie a quick-release knot (see page 11). Trekking ponies gener-

An instructor demonstrates how to mount while eager pupils watch in anticipation of the day's events.

ally wear headcollars or halters all day so that they can be tied up easily at the lunch-time break. In some centres, the bit, with reins attached, is clipped on to the side metal pieces of the headcollar so that the headcollar forms the headpiece and noseband of the bridle. In other centres a bridle – generally without a noseband – is put on over the headcollar. Trekking ponies will nearly always be ridden in snaffle bits. Since the ride never goes faster than a trot the chances of riders being unable to control their pony in a mild bit are slight and, equally, the ponies' mouths will suffer less from the occasional rough handling of a beginner.

Besides the quick-release knot used for tying up the pony, you must also know how to tie the rope of the head-collar around the pony's neck in such a way as to ensure that it does not come undone while you are out on the trek.

The instructors will give you a talk and demonstration on grooming the ponies, showing you how to pick out their feet, sponge the eyes, nostrils and dock, and how to brush the coat, mane and tail. This done, each of you will be allocated your pony for a week, together with a set of grooming equipment. Then you groom your pony. Never be afraid of asking the instructor

Camargue ponies at a trekking centre in Southern France wait patiently to receive their riders.

of any procedure or action you are not sure about. After all, the chances are you have no previous knowledge of how to groom a pony, so all you know is what you have just seen demonstrated – and watching it being done and doing it yourself are two quite different things. The instructors will be present all the time you are grooming and will be only too happy to answer questions or to show you something again.

Tack technique

When grooming is complete, you will have another demonstration – this time on how to tack up your pony. The instructor is likely to stress the importance of putting on tack correctly,

making sure there are no wrinkles in saddle blankets, that girths are not twisted or pinching the skin and so on. This is of particular importance to the ponies in trekking centres. The ponies wear their tack for considerably longer periods than most other ponies – right through the trekking season, which generally stretches from early spring to autumn, for perhaps as much as eight hours a day, six days a week. It is essential to avoid saddle sores and girth galls, for this will put a pony out of action. Tack incorrectly put on can cause these just as quickly as ill-fitting tack, so do make sure for your pony's sake that an instructor checks the saddle after you have done up the

girths. In deference to the ponies' mouths, the instructors or trained staff may well put the bridles on the ponies themselves although they will, of course, show you how to do this if you are interested.

After this you will be shown how to take off the tack which, again, you will do. By now you will find it is nearing lunch-time, so the ponies will be tied up and watered and you will probably have a picnic lunch, which is usually given to you in the morning when you leave the place where you are staying.

How to mount

After lunch, having tacked up the ponies, comes the practical demonstration on how to mount, sit correctly in the saddle, hold the reins, ask the pony to walk forward, turn to the left and right and how to stop and dismount. The instructor will show you this in the schooling area of one of the centre's fields and, the demonstration over, it will then be your turn.

Again, do not be afraid of asking if there is anything you do not under-

stand or any point you have missed in the demonstration. Far better to ask than to find yourself sitting back to front in the saddle. Yes, even that can happen!

After this comes a riding lesson with you in the saddle. What is taught will depend a little on your standard. Complete beginners will work at achieving a good position and seat in the saddle at a halt and walk. Those with a little more experience may be asked to do various exercises so that the instructors can judge each rider's ability. Remember, the main aim of the instructors is not to turn you into a first-class horseman or horsewoman within one week, but rather to ensure that you are sufficiently competent and relaxed in the saddle to enjoy the treks. For this reason, instruction will not be given on more advanced riding techniques such as jumping.

After the lesson, which will probably go on for an hour or so, riders and ponies will return to the yard, where untacking and after-ride grooming is done. At this point the instructor will

probably stress the importance of checking for any signs of saddle sores. The ponies will be watered and fed, if this is being done, all of which will be supervised or undertaken by the centre's staff. While the ponies are feeding you will be given a demonstration of tack cleaning, so that you can then clean your tack.

Trekking centres

All that remains is for the ponies to be turned out into their fields, which may involve leading or herding them to the approved pastures. At some centres this will be undertaken entirely by the staff. At others, visitors are encouraged to help, perhaps by opening gates or blocking junctions to stop the ponies heading off in the wrong direction if they are being herded.

Then you will return to your living

RIGHT: Grooming after removing tack and, below, these young trekkers are being shown how to remove their saddles from their ponies after a hard day's trekking.

A steep incline should be taken slowly, with a rest halfway up if the leaders feel this necessary.

quarters for a welcome bath or shower and the evening meal.

Most trekking centres organize some sort of evening entertainment or are prepared to do so if visitors so wish. This will generally take the form of a demonstration or lecture, or possibly one evening a quiz or some other form of competition. These sessions will normally be related to some aspect of horses and ponies, perhaps going deeper into looking after them under various conditions, or perhaps a talk on some special breed such as Thoroughbreds or Arabs. Since many trekking centres breed their own ponies a talk may be given on this or the routine and training techniques of a big racing stable or on how to break-in and train young horses and ponies. Depending on the facilities at the centre, these talks may be illustrated with films or slides.

Marks for grooming

Many centres will be only too happy to receive suggestions from guests if there are any particular subjects they would like to hear about. Again, do not be afraid to speak out.

Tuesday When you arrive at the centre on the morning of day two, you will be able to get straight on with the grooming of your pony and with putting on his tack. In many centres the instructors will award marks for the pony's cleanliness after your grooming and the daily totals are added up in the form of a little competition, for which a small prize may be awarded at the end of the holiday.

The morning is then taken up with a trek. Incidentally, no trek should have more than twenty riders and if there are this many there should be two instructors accompanying the ride. Smaller numbers of about ten or twelve are better since too large a ride can so easily get out of hand. It also means a very long line of riders for a motorist to pass.

On the subject of roads, most trekking centres try to ride over fields, woodland or open moorland country as much as possible but in almost all areas some road work is unavoidable. It should, however, always consist of minor roads. Your instructor will

advise you how to ride on the roads and you should follow these instructions to the letter. They will have been devised to ensure the maximum possible safety for you and for the other riders. Road work is likely to be conducted at a walk at all times and you should keep in close single file, tucking yourself well into the side of the road.

Follow instructions

You should, of course, follow the instructor's directions all the time you are out on a trek. The instructor will decide when or if the ride should trot, so do not think you know better and ask if you can go faster when you feel like it. Spare a thought for your fellow trekkers who may not be as confident as you. Similarly, if the instructor asks you to

dismount and lead your pony over particularly steep and stony ground or across a rickety bridge, do so without complaining. You can ask why if you like, providing you do so with genuine interest rather than from a wish to query the instructor's decisions.

Many ponies will try to take advantage of having a beginner on their backs to pull at juicy-looking leaves in the hedgerows or at a clump of grass by the side of the road. Try not to let your pony do this. It is a bad habit and if he is allowed to get away with it he will try it on during every ride. It also makes the bit dirty and unpleasant.

Keeping together

Be courteous and friendly to people you meet out trekking. It may just be the farmer whose land you are riding over. Never strike off on a little trail of your own away from the line of riders. Not only will this disorganize the ride but you might be riding over a newly-sown crop without realizing it.

In many trekking centres, on this day the first trek will be for half a day only, to let you 'into the saddle' a little more gently. You will, therefore, return to the centre to have your picnic lunch. On arrival you will follow the now familiar procedure of untacking and grooming your pony. You will be shown how to look over the pony to check that he has not collected any minor injuries, small cuts or scratches out on the ride, and also how to check his shoes in case he needs attention from the farrier.

After lunch you may either have further riding instruction in the form of a lesson in the field or perhaps a lecture and practical demonstration on stable management – how to muck out and strap a pony thoroughly (see page 68). Or perhaps a demonstration on preparing a pony for a show – shampooing the tail, washing the legs and plaiting the mane.

Some trekking centres plunge you in at the deep end a little more quickly and day two is, instead, a full-day's trek. In this case you will stop for an hour or so at an appointed place half way through the day for lunch. At this point the ponies are tied up, their girths slackened off a few holes and the stirrup irons run up the leathers. Some centres

recommend taking off the saddles and bridles altogether for the lunch-time break, in which case they must be put well out of the way of the ponies so that they do not get kicked or trampled on.

Stay well away from the ponies during the lunch-time break unless, of course, any trouble requiring attention breaks out. Essentially they are best left in peace. They have carried you all the morning and are faced with the prospect of doing so again all the afternoon. They need their midday break every bit as much as you do, if not more so.

If you are picnicking do not leave any litter in your wake when you leave. If you do you will be giving pony trekkers a bad name. Remember, too, when you are riding that sudden or loud noises upset horses and ponies very easily. If you want to talk to one of your companions, do so in a moderate voice. Do not shout. If he or she is too far away to hear you unless you shout, wait until you get closer. At the end of the day, when you return to the yard – however stiff and sore you may feel – remember to reward your pony with a pat and a kindly word of thanks for having carried you all day. Evening activities will be similar to those of the previous day.

Wednesday, Thursday and Friday These days usually follow the same procedure – a full day's trek. Morning and evening care of your pony, grooming, tacking up, after-ride care and tack cleaning, will all be done in the same way each day. It will be your responsibility to make sure your pony is still suffering no ill effects from saddle sores, worn or loose shoes or minor injuries. If you notice anything out of the ordinary, tell your instructor.

Average distance

How far you go on a day's trek can vary considerably according to the type of country and the age and experience of the riders. Even the number of people on a ride can affect the distance since smaller groups generally move faster than larger ones. In general, about 16 kilometres (10 miles) will be sufficient for the first couple of days, perhaps working up to about 27–30 kilometres (17–18 miles) by the end of the week.

Some trekking centres organize different activities for Thursday (day four of the holiday) to give both ponies and

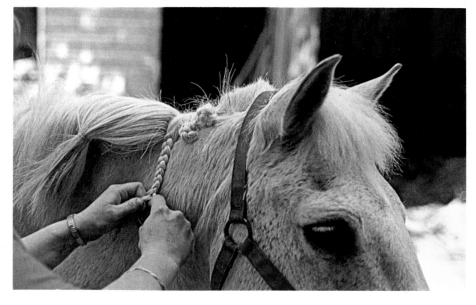

ABOVE: An eager competitor hops home in the sack race – a perennial favourite at all gymkhanas. BELOW: A pony has his mane plaited for a gymkhana at the end of a trekking holiday.

riders a bit of a rest. This could take a number of forms, depending on the facilities in the area. It may include sailing or fell- or hill-walking or perhaps a visit to a nearby beauty spot or place of historic interest. If there is a big stud farm or some racing stables in the area, the owners may have an arrangement to allow the trekkers to be shown round. This is just something else to consider when you book your holiday.

Evening activities for these three days will follow the same procedure as on Monday and Tuesday.

Saturday Different trekking centres organize the final day of the holiday in different ways but some kind of organized competition is usual – often light-hearted gymkhana games. Most of the morning will be spent preparing the pony for this with a specially thorough grooming, and perhaps plaiting the mane, to make him look really smart.

Some centres offer tuition throughout the week for riders interested in elementary dressage movements. The end result of this is a dressage test conducted on the last morning. This is a fairly simple test (the most elementary dressage test drawn up by the Pony Club is usually followed) and participants are marked by the instructor. Centres that include this as part of the week's programme do not make it a compulsory activity.

Gymkhana games

The gymkhana games will include all those events usually found in the programme at local gymkhanas – bending races (weaving in and out along a straight line of poles), musical sacks (a mounted version of the well-known party game of musical chairs), follow-my-leader games and so on. When these are finished there is usually a grand prize-giving session, at which the marked dressage sheets, rosettes for the games, and prizes for the best-groomed pony through the week are given.

If you are not interested in gymkhana games it is often possible to spend the final day trekking as usual.

Depending on the centre – and also on how far away the guests live – some people may leave to go home that evening. Others may find it more convenient to stay on and to travel the following morning.

Rough country

If you only want to trek over a weekend, then much less theoretical instruction, particularly about pony care, will be given. Of course, you will be shown how to mount, sit in the saddle, hold the reins and so on, but less emphasis will be put on how to groom your pony. At weekend treks it is unlikely that the trekkers will be involved much in the care of the pony. They will, of course, be shown how to tie the headcollar rope round the pony's neck and how to tie a quick-release knot, how to tighten the girth and how to slacken it off for the lunch-time break, how to run the stirrup irons up the leathers and how to lead the pony. The instructor will probably emphasize that, in dealing with ponies, doing such things as tightening girths, leading the pony forwards – even mounting and dismounting – are all done from the pony's left side or nearside.

Never attempt to do more than is

asked or expected of you by the instructor, even if you do know how to groom and tack up a pony and want to help. The centre will be organized to include these things in the timetable of the staff and any 'help' from you is more likely to be an interference that will disrupt the centre's smooth operation and running.

If you are a little bit more experienced as a rider and feel you would like to take a riding holiday where the

Young trekkers in hard hats and anoraks sit proudly astride their ponies as they leave the yard for the day's ride ahead.

trekking is more concentrated – that is, where you ride out for longer each day and camp out *en route* over night – do make sure you really are fit enough and that you are also a proficient rider. Such treks usually have to cross rough country at some stage of the route and it may mean you have to do a lot of dismounting and leading your pony. The leaders or instructors on such rides will often ask that you lead your pony for a short distance after a couple of hours of solid riding to relieve his back for a while. There will be other occasions when leading is necessary – perhaps if you are going up or down a very steep and stony hill or if you have to

cross a fast-moving stream, hopping from boulder to boulder while you lead the pony.

Those muscles

If the ponies are being tethered at night you will be shown how to do this and also what to do if the pony injures himself during the ride. But you should really have some knowledge of basic pony care yourself. And above all, you must be used to riding fairly regularly. Even a short trek of, say, three days will render you almost unable to move unless the muscles used in riding have received some preparation for such an ordeal.

8 Riding breeds

There are more than two hundred breeds of horses and ponies in the world today. Some are used by man to help him in his daily work. Many more are used for riding purposes and that covers a myriad of different activities from gentle, recreational hacking to advanced and highly competitive fields of horsemanship such as racing and show jumping. A very few horses still live in herds in the wild.

Of these different breeds, some are native or indigenous to a particular area or country. They have been living there for countless generations, the fittest successively surviving to perpetuate the breed. Other breeds have been produced by man as a result of careful selective interbreeding between types to produce animals that would meet some fashion or requirement – perhaps to move faster, pull heavier loads or to carry greater weights. Nowadays, too, many of the native breeds are also bred in controlled conditions as well as being allowed to breed in the wild. This is because they have proved themselves valuable in so many different ways that they are widely sought after for domestic purposes.

Measurements

The difference between horses and ponies is essentially one of size, although there are said to be some 'pony' characteristics of appearance. Horses and ponies are measured from the ground to the withers in units known as 'hands' – a hand measuring 10 cm (4 in). If an animal measures 13 hands from the ground to its withers, this is traditionally written as 13 h.h. – standing for hands high. If the animal comes between 13 and 14 hands high, the measurement is written as 13.1 h.h. or 13.2 h.h., the last figure measuring 2.5 cm (1 in) or 5 cm (2 in). Animals measuring 14.2 h.h. or less are ponies; those 14.3 h.h. and over are horses.

It would be impossible to discuss all, or even nearly all, the different breeds

The ponies of the Camargue region in Southern France live in very marshy surroundings.

Welsh Mountain ponies have lived wild for centuries.

in detail in this book so we will look at some of the best-known breeds used for popular riding.

Among the most favoured of children's riding ponies are the nine native breeds found in Great Britain. These are the Exmoor, the Dartmoor and the New Forest ponies found in the areas of south and south-west England from which they take their names, the Fells and the Dales, emanating from the western and eastern side of the Pennine range of hills respectively, the Highland from Scotland, the diminutive Shetland from the Shetland and Orkney Isles, the Welsh Mountain from Wales and the Connemara from County Galway in Ireland.

Although all these ponies have their own characteristics, they have many general features in common. Hundreds of years of fending for themselves against harsh weather conditions and an often hostile environment have

made them all hardy, bold and courageous with great stamina and powers of endurance. They also have an inherent intelligence coupled with a certain animal cunning. Because the environment of each one contains rough or stony ground, treacherous narrow tracks or perhaps marshes and hidden bogs, all are incredibly nimble and sure-footed and all appear to possess an in-built knowledge of the local terrain. In addition, all are able to survive on incredibly sparse and meagre rations.

Native breeds

The Exmoor is considered to be the oldest of all Britain's native breeds. It generally stands between 11.2–12.2 h.h., although stallions may be 12.3 h.h., and it has a small, neat head with short, particularly pointed ears and big, brown eyes. Its most notable characteristic is the 'mealy' colour of its muzzle. This is a sort of sandy shade, sometimes also found on the tummy and inner thighs, and is considerably

Note the long mane, tail and forelock of this Shetland pony – all characteristics of the breed.

lighter than the rest of the coat, which is usually brown or dark bay (reddish brown). The Exmoor is renowned for making an excellent riding pony and good jumper, provided it is trained from an early age. It is also much sought after as a foundation stock for mating with other breeds to produce quality riding ponies and hunters.

The Dartmoor is the Exmoor's nearest relative, inhabiting the Devon moors a little to the west. The breed as a whole has suffered over the years from the fact that other horse and pony breeds have often been turned out on the moors, too, and have extensively interbred with the true Dartmoors. As a result, successively fewer and fewer pure bred Dartmoor ponies inhabited the moor and the breed began to show great variations in type. Efforts have been made in recent years to re-establish the breed and to standardize on type. The true Dartmoor is generally stockier in build than the Exmoor, possessing a small head and a strong, well-muscled neck, back and hindquarters. Its maximum height of 12.2 h.h.,

coupled with its kind and sensible temperament, make it an ideal first pony for a young child.

The same vagaries of breeding apply to the New Forest pony since over the years its home area has been grazing land for many different breeds of horse and pony. Thus, although it is known that ponies frequented this area as long ago as a thousand years, they were probably quite different in appearance from those seen grazing in the shady glades of the New Forest today. The New Forest pony is one of the largest of the native breeds, standing anything between 12–14.2 h.h., and it has an extremely willing and placid disposition. The outstanding feature of the breed, however, and one that makes it much sought after as a child's riding pony, is its docile acceptance, and apparent lack of fear, of traffic. This stems from the fact that it is used to cars and lorries roaring past as it grazes on the grassy verges of the forest roads.

The Fells and Dales ponies resemble each other quite closely in appearance, except that the Dales pony is slightly bigger and stockier. Both are dark coloured – often jet black – but they can be dark bay or brown. White markings are frowned upon since these are usually a sign of cross breeding somewhere in the lineage. In former days, the ponies were the mainstay of the local farmers, who used them for all manner

Icelandic ponies are among the hardiest and the friendliest of all the native pony breeds.

of work. They were also used as pack ponies during the seventeenth and eighteenth centuries to carry lead from the inland mines to the ports. The advent of motorization did much to change the lives of these ponies. They were no longer needed to the same extent and their future looked rather bleak for some time. They were saved mainly by the upsurge of interest in pony trekking, for which their quiet nature and inborn knowledge of the country make them ideal.

The sturdy Highland pony is a renowned weight-carrier, traditionally used by deer hunters to carry the deer carcasses down from the hills and mountains after a day's hunting. In addition, it has long helped the small farmers and crofters in their daily work. Two types of Highland pony are recognized – the Western Isles and the Mainland.

The Mainland is the bigger of the

two, usually standing about 14.2 h.h., while the Western Isles may be anything from 12.2–13.2 h.h. Highland ponies may be any colour (piebald and skewbald ones will not be recognized as pure bred by the breed society), although at one time they were nearly always a shade of dun with black mane, tail, lower legs and dorsal stripe. An unusual feature of the coat colouring, particularly apparent in some of the Western Isles types, was the abundance of silver hairs that intermingled throughout the coat, but especially with the black mane and tail.

The Shetland

The tiny Shetland is the smallest of Britain's native breeds and also the strongest in relation to its size. It should not exceed 10.2 h.h. and it has been estimated that it is capable of pulling twice its own weight, whereas most other breeds are considered capable of

pulling loads equivalent to their own weight only. Ancestors of today's Shetland have inhabited the Shetland Islands to the north of Scotland for more than two thousand years and it is thought that the breed has changed little in appearance during that time. Over the centuries the Shetland has been used as a pack and saddle animal as well as being driven in harness and used extensively down in the mines as a pit pony. Nowadays it is chiefly used as a child's first pony and as a family pet.

The Shetland pony may be any

The pretty Gotland pony, known also as the Skogruss pony, is excellent for riding.

colour, including piebald and skewbald, and is characterized by its compact, but thickset, body. It has a profuse mane and tail. The forelock often completely covers its eyes while the full tail sweeps the ground. Its summer coat is fine and glossy but in the winter it grows the thickest, woolliest coat of any breed to protect it from the harsh winter weather that rages across the barren islands.

Welsh Mountain ponies

The pretty Welsh Mountain pony stands about 12 h.h. and is considered by many to be the most attractive of all native ponies. It has inhabited the Welsh hills since the time of the Roman

occupation and has been used ever since as foundation stock for the Welsh pony Sections B and C and the Welsh Cob, all of which are now recognized as different breeds established in their own right, possessing their own stud book. Ponies in Section B resemble the Welsh Mountain pony in appearance but are bigger, standing 12–13.2 h.h. Section C and the Welsh Cob are both stockier in build than the others. The ponies in Section C must not exceed 13.2 h.h. while Welsh Cobs are generally 14–15.1 h.h.

Welsh Mountain ponies are sought after all over the world as children's riding ponies – a job at which they excel in spite of their natural high-spirits.

The dun colouring of the Connemara was once the commonest colour of this breed.

The breed has a small neat head which somewhat resembles that of the Arab (see page 151) in appearance, having a slightly concave profile, together with small, neat ears and large, widely set-apart eyes. Its body is neat and compact, although strong, and its legs are short, but fine. It also often displays the high tail carriage that is characteristic of the Arab and it does indeed have the blood of this breed in its ancestry.

The Connemara

The Connemara is another extremely attractive pony, standing 13–14.2 h.h., although it is considered that the best representatives of the breed stand no higher than 13.2 h.h. Although once much used as a pack and harness pony, it is as a child's riding pony that it is now most widely sought after and acclaimed. Because of this there have been various attempts in recent years to 'improve' the breed by introducing small Thoroughbred stal-

lions and part Arabs. This, in turn, has led to various changes in the appearance and characteristics of the breed, although those still living in the rather poor pastures of their native homeland continue to breed true to type. The characteristic colouring was dun with black dorsal stripe, legs, mane and tail, but this is now seen less and less frequently.

Other native ponies much used in their home countries for riding purposes are the Gotland, from the island of the same name lying off the southeast coast of Sweden, the Icelandic pony, the Fjord pony, originating in Norway but found throughout Scandinavia, the Haflinger from Austria and the Camargue from Southern France. All are used by the local inhabitants, particularly by farmers and homesteaders, as work animals as well as riding and family ponies. But apart from this the main use of all these ponies is for trekking. Trekking holidays are features of all these areas.

The Gotland pony, standing 12–12.2 h.h., is known also as the Skogruss and

is an ancient breed, claimed to be a descendant of one of the prehistoric types of pony. It is thought to be the oldest of all the Scandinavian breeds, but over the centuries it has interbred with other breeds, in particular the Arab. It has long been in demand to help the island farmers in doing light work around the farms and more recently has found much favour as a children's riding pony. It is good at and enjoys jumping and its energetic action at the trot has led to its being used competitively in harness trotting races.

Icelandic

The little Icelandic pony is one of the toughest of all breeds of native pony. Ancestors of the breed were apparently taken to Iceland by the Norsemen who settled on the island during the ninth and tenth centuries. They would have transported the ponies across the rough seas in their long boats, and the fact that they survived this is testimony to their endurance and stamina. For centuries, the Icelandic ponies were the only forms of transport on the island, and even today much of the country is

unsuitable for motor vehicles, so the ponies are still used as pack and draught animals. As cattle cannot survive the cold Icelandic winters, the ponies have also been bred as a source of meat for the islanders.

Standing 12–13 h.h., these ponies are among the most naturally docile and friendly of all native ponies. So willing and responsive are they that they can generally be trained to act upon commands from their rider's voice only. They possess an unusual, but well developed, homing instinct which makes them ideal for trekkers who lose their way or for local people who want to go on a one-way journey yet return the pony to its home.

The Fjord pony is another ancient breed, probably related to the Icelandic pony, although it is a little larger and heavier. It is still widely used as a working animal by farmers in hilly areas throughout northern Europe – Denmark and Germany in particular. It appears to be unaffected by cold conditions and is renowned for its constant willingness and friendly, hardworking nature. When used as a riding pony it is a good weight-carrier.

The Fjord is almost always a shade of dun and often displays 'bar' or stripey black markings on its legs. These are usually signs of primitive ancestry. Its coarse mane is generally trimmed to stand erect from its neck along the crest and usually comprises a central stripe of black hairs flanked either side by silver ones. The tail, too, is a mixture of black and silver hairs.

Austrian Haflinger

The Austrian Haflinger is a native of the mountain pastures of the South Tyrol. Although it is an old breed, it has been improved over the last few decades and now contains considerable Arab blood, which shows in its appearance. It has been used in agricultural and forestry work and is remarkably strong for its height, which is up to about 14 h.h. However, it also makes an excellent riding pony, particularly for riding along the mountain tracks, where it is amazingly sure-footed. The

Dartmoor ponies have their meagre winter grazing supplemented by a ration of hay.

Haflinger ponies playing together in the snow. They are renowned for hard work.

Haflinger is renowned for living to a great age. It is usually a bright chestnut colour with a flaxen mane and tail.

The pretty Camargue is another ancient breed, descended from prehistoric horses and later interbred with various Eastern horses. The Camargues are found in the marshy region of the Rhone delta of Southern France – a watery home they share with the equally famous black bulls of the Camargue. They are widely used in riding schools and trekking centres in the area and are also the mounts of the cowboys

or 'gardians' of the Camargue, who use them to patrol the marshes and to round up the bulls at various times of the year, perhaps for branding or for sale. The rigours of the habitat have made them hardy, surefooted and full of stamina. They are also noted for their fiery, independent temperament.

The Camargue is almost invariably grey. The foals are born black but the coat gets progressively lighter with each successive moult. They seldom exceed 14 h.h. when fully matured.

Probably the most famous breed of riding horse, originally developed in Great Britain but now bred all over the world, is the Thoroughbred. This magnificent animal owes its origin to man's

interest in and love of racing, which, although it has been a popular sport since time immemorial, only became fashionable and respectable in the late seventeenth century when it gained royal patronage. In consequence, the Thoroughbred emerged as a breed round about the beginning of the eighteenth century.

The Thoroughbred

The Thoroughbred ranges in height from about 15–17 h.h. and is the most elegant of horses, with a refined head and neck, compact but deep body and long, clean, slender legs. Although primarily bred for racing (a sport it now pursues in more than fifty count-

ries), it also makes a superb riding horse and excels in many other types of competition such as show jumping and three-day eventing. It is also extensively used as foundation stock to improve other breeds and types of horse and pony.

The horse mainly responsible for the development of the Thoroughbred was one that is still widely sought after as a superb riding horse – the Arab. It has been living in the deserts of Arabia for centuries and is now another breed that is favoured and fostered the world over, to the extent that breeding centres are established in all major countries. Many people consider this to be the most beautiful of all horses and it has

done more than any other breed of horse or pony to establish and to help to develop new breeds or to upgrade those already in existence.

The Arab

The nomadic Bedouins fully realized the value of their Arab horses and guarded them jealously, often going without food themselves rather than let their horses go hungry if rations were short. The origins of the breed are obscure, although the subject of much myth and romantic legend as well as continual disagreement among the experts.

Although there are numbers of different types of Arab, varying slightly in

The Thoroughbred was created to satisfy man's desire for speed. It is also known as the racehorse.

appearance, all possess certain features in common. They have small, refined, clean-boned heads with a concave profile (known as a dished nose), small neat ears, large, widely set-apart eyes and a small, perfectly shaped muzzle. The neck is long and elegantly arched and the mane long and flowing. The body is neat and compact but well-muscled and strong and the legs are clean and finely boned. The tail is full and characteristically carried rather high. The action of the Arab is amazingly free and flowing, almost as if floating on the air.

A quality riding horse results when Thoroughbreds and Arabs are crossed. This has become known as the Anglo-Arab and it, too, is bred in many countries, principally in France, Great Britain and Poland. It usually stands between 15.2–16 h.h. and often possesses great jumping ability. This has led to its finding success in many competitive sports as well as to being sought after as a hunter.

The United States has many fine breeds of riding horse, all developed within the last two hundred years.

The beautiful Arab is bred in most horse-loving countries of the world. This one is from Morocco.

Among the most famous is the American Saddle Horse or Saddlebred, developed originally in Kentucky and still bred mainly there and in Virginia. It is a horse of extremely distinguished appearance with lively, energetic action. Most Saddlebreds are trained in a further couple of gaits in addition to the walk, trot and canter. These are the slow gait and the 'rack'. The slow gait is a pace in four-time in which each foot is placed on the ground separately, seeming to pause in mid-air before doing so. This makes it extremely graceful to watch. The rack is essentially the same action but is performed at great speed. The Saddlebred is mainly bred as a show horse.

Another American breed with an unusual gait is the Tennessee Walking Horse, developed by plantation owners in Tennessee who wanted a horse that above all else would give them a comfortable ride. An elegant-looking horse, standing 15.2–16 h.h., the Tennessee Walking Horse has a gait described as a 'running walk', which again is a pace in four-time. It is claimed this pace cannot be taught successfully to any other breed, although it has become almost inbred in the Tennessee Walking Horse. It is a steady, gliding pace which covers a lot of ground with each stride.

The horse most frequently used by the cowboys and ranch hands in their daily work with cattle and in rodeo

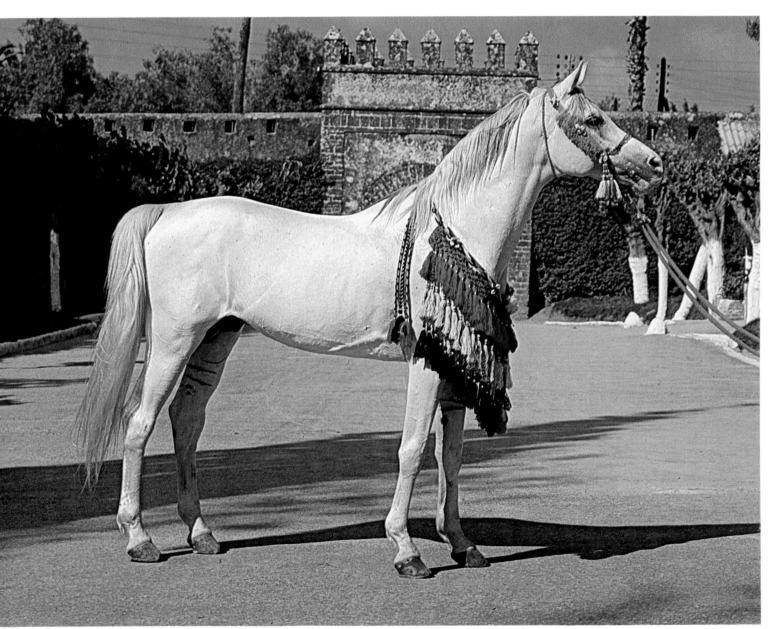

competitions is the Quarter Horse. This is said to possess inherent 'cow sense'. It seems to know what it should do in any situation, before receiving instructions from its rider. To this end, too, it is amazingly agile and fast and yet is able to come to an immediate halt, even from a gallop, or to spin around in the space of its own length. These attributes have also made it widely sought after as a polo pony. Its name is derived from the popular sport of 'match racing' indulged in by the early colonial settlers and for which the breed was primarily developed. These were short races, often run in the main street of the town and usually over a distance of about a quarter of a mile.

Ireland has long been the home of quality riding horses and the Irish are renowned as judges of horse flesh. So successful and sought-after are their horses that the Irish Hunter has come to be recognized internationally as a breed, although a hunter is essentially a type of horse rather than a breed. The term is used to describe any horse suitable for riding to hounds and its height and physique will vary according to the weight of the rider and the type of country being hunted. However, certain features are recognized as being characteristic of hunters to the extent that most large horse shows include several classes for hunters of various types.

The Irish Hunter, which usually stands between 16–16.3 h.h., was developed from crossing Irish mares – particularly those of the well-built but active and energetic Irish Draught Horse – with Thoroughbred stallions. The result is a bold, long-striding animal, usually possessing the qualities of speed, endurance and an ability to jump.

The stocky Irish Cob is another breed of note, bred principally as a harness horse, but also highly successful as a saddle horse for heavyweight rid-

The high head and tail carriage are characteristics of the aristocratic American Saddlebred.

Travelling in grand style. The famous Lipizzaner horses used by the Spanish riding school of Vienna.

ers. It has good action, is kind, sensible and seemingly tireless.

France, Sweden and Germany, in particular, are all justifiably renowned for their riding horses. In all these countries the breeding of horses is controlled by the government and the aim appears to be to cross regional breeds with one another to produce a national

saddle horse of outstanding quality.

The French Saddle Horse, or Selle Français, is the name that has recently been given to this type of horse produced by the French, which has shown itself to be highly successful in three-day eventing and show jumping. In fact, the name embraces a number of regional breeds of similar appearance and standard, such as the Anglo-Norman – a breed originally developed by crossing native, heavily-built mares with imported stock including Thoroughbreds. In the past these

horses have found favour as coach and cavalry horses. The French Saddle Horse stands 15.2–16.2 h.h. and is generally bay or chestnut, although it can be any colour.

Germany has many fine regional breeds, such as the Hanoverian, the Trakehner, the Holstein, the Oldenburg and others. Many of these are similar in appearance and performance and are designated their breed name according to their birthplace. Obviously they are subject to regional variation and the breeds also have

differing histories of development, but the aim now – and one that top class international competition results have shown to be justified – is to produce a powerful, good-tempered, bold riding horse able to compete successfully in eventing and show jumping.

The Swedish Halfbred or Warmblood, a horse of great ability, excels particularly in dressage and is bred at the national stud at Flyinge in Sweden. It has been developed primarily from crosses of Thoroughbreds, Oriental breeds of horse and German horses.

The type that has emerged is a tall horse, standing 16–16.2 h.h. with superb conformation and movement and an intelligent, tractable nature. Quality is strictly controlled at the stud. Only those animals that are successful in passing a series of tests are kept for the purposes of breeding.

White Lippizzaners

Finally, a word about one of the best known riding horses of all, the beautiful white Lipizzaners of the Spanish Riding School of Vienna. These magni-

ficent animals have been bred in Austria since a stud was established there in 1580 and all the horses at the school today are descended from six strains of Lipizzaner established there soon after.

Lipizzaners are the doyens of haute école – the most advanced form of dressage training and discipline for both horse and rider. The superb white stallions are world-famous and, indeed, travel all over the world to give exhibitions of their faultlessly executed, beautifully timed movements.

155

Glossary

aids signals used by the rider to communicate with, and control, his horse. 'Natural' aids are the hands, body, legs and voice.

artificial aids ancillary equipment which helps the rider to control his horse; includes whips, sticks, spurs and items of tack such as martingales.

basculating the action of a horse as he balances his body over the centre of a jump.

bit that part of a bridle placed directly in the horse's mouth, attached to the reins. It is usually made of metal, and its purpose is to give the rider greater control over the horse's mouth than he would otherwise have.

cast term given to a horse or pony lying down in the stable and unable to get up owing to lack of space or because he is pressed up against a wall.

cavaletti long wooden poles attached at either end to short crossed planks in such a way that they can be placed on the ground to stand at three different heights. They are used for jumping training and practice.

draw reins reins attached to the girth and passing through the bit rings to the rider's hands. They are a very severe and corrective form of control.

dressage the art of classical equitation, that is, training a horse in certain recognized school movements that require discipline, obedience and skill.

farrier a person who shoes horses and ponies. The name was originally used to describe someone in the army who looked after sick horses and mules under instruction from a veterinary surgeon.

fillet string plaited braid attached to either side of the back part of a summer sheet. It passes under the horse's tail and prevents the rug blowing up in a breeze.

gymkhana a small, informal, local show in which riders and ponies compete in mounted games.

hack term used both to describe going out for a recreational ride and a particular type of horse.

horse equine that stands over 14.2 hands high. (A hand equals 100 cm (4 in) and is the recognized unit of measure for horses and ponies.)

jodhpur specially tailored, close-fitting riding trousers which reach down to the ankle (as opposed to breeches which come to the knee and are worn with long boots).

loose box stabling for a horse or pony which comprises a self-contained 'room' where the animal does not need to be tied up.

to lunge to lead a horse round in a circle on a long rein. The instructor or trainer holds the rein and stands in the centre of the circle.

manège a marked-out rectangular area of ground used for training horses and teaching riders. It can be in an outdoor paddock or within a covered building. The sides are always marked with the letters A, K, E, H, C, M, B and F.

mucking out part of the morning stable routine in which all the bedding soiled during the night is removed and the floor of the stable swept before clean bedding is put down.

nearside the left side of a horse or pony.

New Zealand rug a wool-lined, waterpfoof rug kept in place by a strap at the chest, two long straps that pass round the hind legs and a strap or surcingle that buckles round the animal's middle. It is worn by ponies at grass in the winter—never by those kept in a stable.

offside the right side of a horse or pony.

to overreach to strike the heel of the forefeet with the toes of the hindfeet.

overreach boots rubber 'boots' which fit over the hoofs to protect the forefeet from overreaching.

oxer a spread fence consisting of a hedge flanked on either side by rails.

plaiting arranging the mane in braided knots to give a tidy appearance for shows.

to point (of a horse's forefoot) literally to point the foreleg forward when standing still, so as to take pressure off the foot or leg that is giving the animal pain.

pony equine that stands 14.2 hands high or under.

pony cube commercially prepared food for ponies, consisting of a mixture of various foodstuffs compacted into small cubes or pellets.

quartering quick grooming in which a stabled horse's rugs are not removed; consists of sponging eyes, nostrils and dock and brushing those parts of the coat exposed by lifting the edges of the rug. The purpose is to make the animal look respectable for going out on exercise.

to rein back to ask the horse to move backwards. The movement should be done in a pace of two-time, that is, each pair of diagonal hindlegs and forelegs moving in unison.

side reins reins attached to the bit at one end and, at the other end, either to the girth of the saddle or to a roller buckled round the horse's middle if no saddle is being worn. They are used for training purposes.

spread (fence) an obstacle in a jumping course, built to test the horse's ability to jump width as well as height.

strapping term given to the thorough grooming of a stable-kept horse or pony.

summer sheet a lightweight cotton rug mainly worn by show horses to prevent dust settling on their coats.

tack general term for all items of saddlery. It is an abbreviation of 'tackle', another word for harness.

to tack up to saddle and bridle a horse or pony.

trace clip term given to the practice of clipping off the winter coat along the belly and underneath the neck. This helps to make these areas easier to keep clean in wet, muddy conditions and also stops the animal sweating too profusely if doing heavy work.

trekking organized cross-country riding (usually associated with pony trekking holidays).

turning out term given to letting a horse or pony free in the paddock or field after a period of captivity, for example, to return him to the field after a ride.

upright (fence) an obstacle in a jumping course in which the emphasis is on the height of the fence.

Index

Acknowledgments

The publishers would like to thank the following organizations and individuals for their kind permission to reproduce the photographs in this book:
All special photography by Peter Roberts; Gordon Carlisle: 115, 135, 140 above; Bruce Coleman Ltd: (Mike Price) 145, 158–9, (Hans Reinhard) 4, 142; Bob Langrish: 102 above, 108, 109, 114, 130, 134, 140 below; Jane Miller: 143, 148–9; Sally-Anne Thompson: (Animal Photography) 2–3, 131, 144, 146, 147, 150, 151, 152, 153, 154–5.